♓   THE PISCES ENIGMA   ♓

Cracking the Code

ALSO BY JANE RIDDER-PATRICK

A Handbook of Medical Astrology
Shaping Your Future (Series of 12 titles)
Shaping Your Relationships (Series of 12 titles)

The Zodiac Code series

THE
PISCES
ENIGMA

Cracking the Code

JANE RIDDER-PATRICK

MAINSTREAM
PUBLISHING
EDINBURGH AND LONDON

For our three Hamburg Fische: Malte, Christiane and Oskar, with love

First published in Great Britain in 2004 by
MAINSTREAM PUBLISHING COMPANY
(EDINBURGH) LTD
7 Albany Street
Edinburgh EH1 3UG

ISBN 1 84018 525 2

A catalogue record for this book is available
from the British Library

Typeset in Allise and Van Dijck

Printed in Great Britain by
Cox & Wyman Ltd

Contents

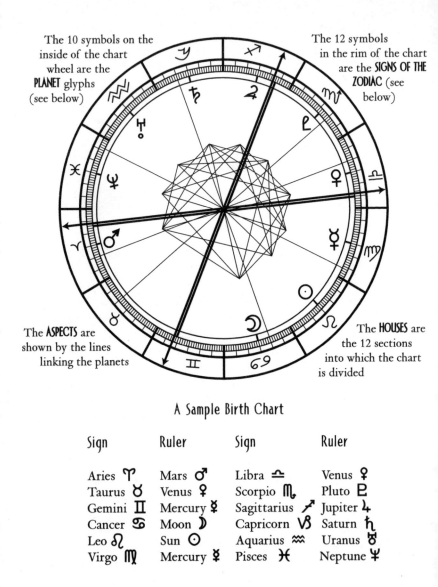

The 10 symbols on the inside of the chart wheel are the **PLANET** glyphs (see below)

The 12 symbols in the rim of the chart are the **SIGNS OF THE ZODIAC** (see below)

The **ASPECTS** are shown by the lines linking the planets

The **HOUSES** are the 12 sections into which the chart is divided

A Sample Birth Chart

Sign	Ruler	Sign	Ruler
Aries ♈	Mars ♂	Libra ♎	Venus ♀
Taurus ♉	Venus ♀	Scorpio ♏	Pluto ♇
Gemini ♊	Mercury ☿	Sagittarius ♐	Jupiter ♃
Cancer ♋	Moon ☽	Capricorn ♑	Saturn ♄
Leo ♌	Sun ☉	Aquarius ♒	Uranus ♅
Virgo ♍	Mercury ☿	Pisces ♓	Neptune ♆

ONE

The Truth of Astrology

MOST PEOPLE'S FIRST EXPERIENCE OF ASTROLOGY IS THROUGH newspapers and magazines. This is a mixed blessing for astrology's reputation – writing an astrology column to any degree of accuracy is a tough, many would say impossible, challenge. The astrologer has to try to say something meaningful about conditions that affect every single person belonging to the same sign, over a very short period of time, in a scant handful of words. The miracle is that some talented astrologers do manage to get across a tantalising whiff of the real thing and keep readers coming back for more of what most of us are hungry for – self-knowledge and reassurance about the future. The downside of the popularity of these columns is that many people think that all astrology is a branch of the entertainment industry and is limited to light-hearted fortune-telling. This is far from the truth.

What Astrology Can Offer

Serious astrology is one of the most sophisticated tools available to help us understand ourselves and the world around us. It gives us a language and a framework to examine and describe – quite literally – *anything* under the Sun, from countries to companies, from money markets to medical matters. Its most common application, however, is in helping people to understand themselves better using their own unique birth charts. Astrology has two main functions. One is to describe the traits and tendencies of whatever it is that is being examined, whether this is a state, a software company or someone's psyche. The other is to give an astonishingly accurate timetable for important changes within that entity. In the chapters that follow, we'll be using astrology to investigate the psychology of the innermost part of your personality, taking a look at what drives, inspires and motivates you.

Astrology uses an ancient system of symbols to describe profound truths about the nature of life on earth, truths that cannot be weighed and measured, but ones we recognise nevertheless, and that touch and move us at a deep level. By linking mythology and mathematics, astrology bridges the gap between our inner lives and our outer experiences, between mind and matter, between poetry and science.

Fate and Free Will

Some people think that astrology is all about foretelling the future, the implication being that everything is predestined and that we have no say in how our lives take shape. None of that is true. We are far from being helpless victims of fate. Everything that happens to us at any given time is the result of past choices. These choices may have been our own, or made by other people. They could even have been made long ago before we, or even our grandparents, were born. It is not always possible to prevent processes that were set in motion in the past from coming to their logical conclusions as events that we then have to deal with. We are, however, all free to decide how to react to whatever is presented to us at every moment of our lives.

Your destiny is linked directly with your personality because the choices you make, consciously or unconsciously, depend largely on your own natural inclinations. It is these inclinations that psychological astrology describes. You can live out every single part of your chart in a constructive or a less constructive way. For instance, if you have Aries strong in your chart, action and initiative will play a major role in your life. It is your choice whether you express yourself aggressively or assertively, heroically or selfishly, and also whether you are the doer or the done-to. Making the right choices is important because every decision has consequences – and what you give out, sooner or later, you get back. If you don't know and understand yourself, you are 'fated' to act according to instinct and how your life experiences have conditioned you. By revealing how you are wired up temperamentally, astrology can highlight alternatives to blind knee-jerk reactions, which often make existing problems worse. This self-knowledge can allow you to make more informed free-will choices, and so help you create a better and more successful future for yourself.

Astrology and Prediction

Astrology cannot predict specific events based on your birth chart. That kind of prediction belongs to clairvoyance and divination. These specialities, when practised by gifted and responsible individuals, can give penetrating insights into events that are likely to happen in the future if matters proceed along their present course.

The real benefit of seeing into the future is that if we don't like what could happen if we carry on the way we're going, we can take steps either to prevent it or to lessen its impact. Rarely is the future chiselled out in stone. There are many possible futures. What you feed with your attention grows. Using your birth chart, a competent astrologer can map out, for years in advance, major turning points, showing which areas of your life will be affected at these times and the kind of change that will be taking place. This information gives answers to the questions that most clients ask in one way or another: 'Why me, why this and why now?' If you accept responsibility for facing what needs to be done at the appropriate time, and doing it, you can change the course of your life for the better.

Astrology and the Soul

What is sometimes called the soul and its purpose is a mystery much more profound than astrology. Most of us have experienced 'chance' meetings and apparent 'tragedies' which have affected the direction of our entire lives. There is an intelligence at work that is infinitely wiser and more powerful than the will or wishes of our small egocentric personalities. This force, whatever name we give it – Universal Wisdom, the Inner Guide, the Self, a guardian angel – steers us into exactly the right conditions for our souls' growth. Astrology can pinpoint the turning points in the course of your destiny and describe the equipment that you have at your disposal for serving, or resisting, the soul's purpose. That equipment is your personality.

Who Are You?

You are no doubt aware of your many good qualities as well as your rather more resistible ones that you might prefer to keep firmly under wraps. Maybe you have wondered why it is that one part of your personality seems to want to do one thing while another part is stubbornly intent on doing the exact opposite. Have you ever wished that you could crack the code that holds the secrets of what makes you – and significant others – behave in the complex way you do? The good news is that you can, with the help of your astrological birth chart, sometimes known as your horoscope.

Just as surely as your DNA identifies you and distinguishes you from everyone else, as well as encoding your peculiarities and potential, your birth chart reveals the unique 'DNA fingerprinting' of your personality. This may seem a staggering claim, but it is one that those who have experienced serious astrology will endorse, so let's take a closer look at what a birth chart is.

Your Birth Chart

Your birth chart is a simplified diagram of the positions of the planets, as seen from the place of your birth, at the moment you took your first independent breath. Critics have said that astrology is obviously nonsense because birth charts are drawn up as if the Sun and all the planets moved round the Earth.

We know in our minds that the Earth moves round the Sun, but that doesn't stop us seeing the Sun rise in the east in the morning and move across the sky to set in the west in the evening. This is an optical illusion. In the same way, we know (or at least most of us know) that we are not really the centre of the universe, but that doesn't stop us experiencing ourselves as being at the focal point of our own personal worlds. It is impossible to live life in any other way. It is the strength, not weakness, of astrology that it describes from your own unique viewpoint how you, as an individual, experience life.

Erecting Your Chart

To draw up a full birth chart you need three pieces of information – the date, time and place of your birth. With your birth date alone you can find the positions of all the planets (except sometimes the Moon) to a good enough degree of accuracy to reveal a great deal of important information about you. If you have the time and place of birth, too, an astrologer can calculate your Ascendant or Rising Sign and the houses of your chart – see below. The Ascendant is a bit like the front door of your personality and describes your general outlook on life. (If you know your Ascendant sign, you might like to read more about its characteristics in the book on that sign in this series.)

The diagram on page 6 shows what a birth chart looks like. Most people find it pretty daunting at first sight but it actually breaks down into only four basic units – the planets, the signs, the aspects and the houses.

The Planets

Below is a simple list of what the planets represent.

PLANET	REPRESENTS YOUR URGE TO
☉ The Sun	express your identity
☽ The Moon	feel nurtured and safe
☿ Mercury	make connections
♀ Venus	attract what you love
♂ Mars	assert your will
♃ Jupiter	find meaning in life
♄ Saturn	achieve your ambitions
♅ Uranus	challenge tradition
♆ Neptune	serve an ideal
♇ Pluto	eliminate, transform and survive

The planets represent the main psychological drives that every single one of us has. The exact way in which we express these drives is not fixed from birth but develops and evolves throughout our lives, both consciously and unconsciously. In this book we will be examining in detail four of these planets – your Sun, Moon, Mercury and Venus. These are the bodies that are right at the heart of our solar system. They correspond, in psychological astrology, to the core of your personality and represent how you express yourself, what motivates you emotionally, how you use your mind and what brings you pleasure.

The Signs
The signs your planets are in show how you tend to express your inner drives. For example, if your Mars is in the action sign of Aries, you will assert yourself pretty directly, pulling no punches. If your Venus is in secretive Scorpio, you will attract, and also be attracted to, emotionally intense relationships. There is a summary of all of the signs on p. 128.

The Aspects
Aspects are important relationships between planets and whether your inner characteristics clash with or complement each other depends largely on whether or not they are in aspect and whether that aspect is an easy or a challenging one. In Chapter Six we'll be looking at some challenging aspects to the Sun.

The Houses
Your birth chart is divided into 12 slices, called houses, each of which is associated with a particular area of life, such as friendships, travel or home life. If, for example, you have your Uranus in the house of career, you are almost

certainly a bit of a maverick at work. If you have your Neptune in the house of partnership, you are likely to idealise your husband, wife or business partner.

The Nature of Time

Your birth chart records a moment in time and space, like a still from a movie – the movie being the apparent movement of the planets round the earth. We all know that time is something that can be measured in precise units, which are always the same, like seconds, months and centuries. But if you stop to reflect for a moment, you'll also recognise that time doesn't always feel the same. Twenty minutes waiting for a bus on a cold, rainy day can seem like a miserable eternity, while the same amount of time spent with someone you love can pass in a flash. As Einstein would say – that's relativity.

There are times in history when something significant seems to be in the air, but even when nothing momentous is happening the quality of time shifts into different 'moods' from moment to moment. Your birth chart is impregnated with the qualities of the time when you were born. For example, people who were born in the mid-to-late 1960s, when society was undergoing major disruptive changes, carry those powerful energies within them and their personalities reflect, in many ways, the turmoil of those troubled and exciting times. Now, as adults, the choices that those individuals make, based on their own inner conflicts and compulsions, will help shape the future of society for better or worse. And so it goes on through the generations.

Seed Meets Soil

There is no such thing as a good or bad chart, nor is any one sign better or worse than another. There are simply 12 different, but equally important, life focuses. It's useful to keep in mind the fact that the chart of each one of us is made up of all the signs of the zodiac. This means that we'll act out, or experience, *every* sign somewhere in our lives. It is true, however, that some individual charts are more challenging than others; but the greater the challenge, the greater the potential for achievement and self-understanding.

In gardening terms, your chart is a bit like the picture on a seed packet. It shows what you could become. If the seeds are of poppies, there's no way you'll get petunias, but external conditions will affect how they grow. With healthy soil, a friendly climate and green-fingered gardeners, the plants have an excellent chance of flourishing. With poor soil, a harsh climate or constant neglect, the seeds will be forced to struggle. This is not always a disadvantage. They can become hardy and adapt, finding new and creative ways of evolving and thriving under more extreme conditions than the plant that was well cared for. It's the same with your chart. The environment you were raised in may have been friendly or hostile to your nature and it will have done much to shape your life until now. Using the insights of astrology to affirm who you are, you can, as an adult, provide your own ideal conditions, become your own best gardener and live out more fully – and successfully – your own highest potential.

TWO

The Symbolism of Pisces

WE CAN LEARN A GREAT DEAL ABOUT PISCES BY LOOKING AT the myths, legends and symbols associated with it. These are time-honoured ways of describing important psychological truths; they carry more information than plain facts alone, and hint at the deeper meanings and significance of the sign.

The Pisces glyph is made up of two upright crescents, facing in opposite directions, joined and intersected by a horizontal straight line. One of the crescents is said to represent the limited waking consciousness available to us as individuals, while the other is the dreamlike cosmic consciousness that connects us with 'all that there is'. The line through them stands for the Earth, where dream and drudgery and the mystical and material aspects of life meet and mingle. It shows the difficult task that Pisceans have of living both in the everyday outer world and in the ethereal inner world of ideals and imagination – and of finding some way of integrating these seemingly irreconcilable realities within themselves.

Pisces the Fish

The symbol for Pisces is made up of two fish swimming in opposite directions, tied to each other by a connecting cord. This echoes the shape of the constellation of Pisces, where one 'fish' swims towards Aries and the other points in the direction of Aquarius, underlining once more the creative tension at the heart of Pisces. One of the fish, swimming downstream, signifies spirit descending into matter and, like Aries, is fully present in the world, ready to fight for and rescue those in trouble. The other fish, swimming upstream, represents the soul making its journey back home and, like Aquarius, stands aloof from the world.

As a Piscean, you can find it difficult to make up your mind about which direction you want to go in. When one part of you wants to go one way, another part always contradicts and tugs you towards the opposite path. These conflicting pulls are a constant source of frustration for most Pisceans, but there's no way that one fish can escape the other. The cord represents the restrictions of destiny, allowing you no easy way out of the dilemma of having one foot in heaven and the other on Earth.

The Rulers of Pisces

Pisces has two planets associated with it – its traditional ruler, Jupiter, and its modern one, Neptune. Astrologers build up a profile of a new-found planet not only by a careful study of its apparent effects over time, but also by examining what was going on in the world when it was discovered. Neptune was discovered in 1846. At this time, spiritualism and seances were becoming popular, and anaesthetics were first used in medicine and in childbirth. Contact with 'higher worlds', suffering and its relief, as well as chemically induced shifts of consciousness, are all important themes of Pisces and Neptune. The first synthetic dye, mauveine, was produced then, too, by a Piscean chemist Henry Perkin, who earned a fortune and a knighthood from it. This development transformed everyday life for even the poorest, as it opened the way for rainbow colours in clothes and furnishings, in place of the subdued, drab hues of vegetable dyes. Interestingly, the colour mauve traditionally symbolises suffering.

In mythology, Neptune ruled the waters of the Earth, and all that was in them. It's a kingdom of breathtaking beauty, with hidden depths and treacherous cross-currents, mists and reflections, peaceful calms and tidal waves. The oceans are inhabited by a fantasia of creatures, and are also the common final resting place for both the world's treasures and trash. Like the oceans, Pisceans have among their ranks the highest and lowliest of humanity, united by the common urge to dissolve their sense of separateness, and to become at one with all.

Pisces shares its other ruler, Jupiter, with Sagittarius. Like you, as a Piscean, Jupiter was an adventurer and gambler, trusting his luck to its limits and venturing into situations where angels would tremble to tread. Jupiter was also a skilled actor and a master of disguise and deception. Pisceans, too, are notable shape-shifters, well able to go with the flow in whatever situations they find themselves.

Pisces in Myth and Legend

The fish is an important symbol in many faiths, representing both worldly and spiritual power. Reflecting this, bishop's mitres are shaped like fish heads. In Hinduism, fish are said to be instruments of revelation and salvation, and are linked with the god Vishnu, the

Preserver. Buddha, like Christ, was known as the 'fisher of men', and among the Celtic peoples the salmon is a symbol of wisdom, foreknowledge and spiritual inspiration. Yet fish are also greedy omnivores, with voracious appetites, and graze constantly. If supplies are unrestricted, they will gorge themselves to the detriment of their own health. Many Pisceans, likewise, find it difficult to know when to stop.

The symbolism of the two linked fish is probably the most confusing and convoluted in the entire zodiac. The pair has been associated with a whole galaxy of deities. Into the melting pot, as contenders for one fish, go the goddesses Ishtar, Isis, Aphrodite and Venus, all of whom have Friday as their day – hence the custom of eating fish on Fridays. The other fish has been linked with Ichthys, or Dagon, the fish god of Babylonia, as well as Horus, Tammuz, Eros, Bacchus the god of wine, Dionysus the saviour and, of course, Christ. The common thread running through all of these is the story of an eternal relationship in which, periodically, either through willing sacrifice or adverse circumstances, one of the pair falls victim to death, madness or dismemberment. There is then a period of mourning for the loss and yearning for reunion, followed by salvation and redemption. Esoterically, this cycle of separation and sorrow, rescue and renewal refers to the pain of choosing – or being forced (depending on your viewpoint) – to incarnate on earth and losing, temporarily, the blissful fusion with the source of all life. The fear of abandonment, as well as a longing to rescue or be rescued from sorrow and suffering, are some of Pisces' most important themes.

Season of Pisces

When the Sun is in Pisces, spring has not yet arrived and winter is not yet over. Lent, the 40 days that lead up to Easter, begins now. At this time, for devout Christians, the eating of meat – except fish – is forbidden and they are expected to sacrifice luxuries to purify their souls. In the past, it was partly a religious festival and partly sheer necessity, as the food reserves which had been stored for the winter were coming to an end and had to be rationed. In the northern hemisphere, late February and March is also a time of hope, when the days lengthen as the year moves on, out of the cold, darkness and restrictions of winter into the salvation of the coming of spring.

THREE

The Heart of the Sun

O THE GLYPH FOR THE SUN IS A PERFECT CIRCLE WITH A DOT in the centre and symbolises our dual nature – earthly and eternal. The circle stands for the boundary of the personality, which distinguishes and separates each individual from every other individual, for it is our differences from other people that make us unique, not our similarities. The dot in the centre indicates the mysterious 'divine spark' within us and the potential for becoming conscious of who we truly are, where we have come from and what we may become.

The Meaning of the Sun

Each of your planets represents a different strand of your personality. The Sun is often reckoned to be the most important factor of your whole birth chart. It describes your sense of identity, and the sign that the Sun was in when you were born, your Sun sign, along with its house position and any aspects to other planets, shows how you express and develop that identity.

Your Role in Life

Each of the signs is associated with certain roles that can be played in an infinite number of ways. Take one of the roles of Aries, which is the warrior. A warrior can cover anything from Attila the Hun, who devastated vast stretches of Europe with his deliberate violence, to an eco-warrior, battling to save the environment. The role, warrior, is the same; the motivation and actions are totally different. You can live out every part of your personality in four main ways – as creator, destroyer, onlooker or victim. How you act depends on who you choose to be from the endless variations possible from the symbolism of each of your planets, but most particularly your Sun. And you do have a choice; not all Geminis are irresponsible space cadets nor is every Scorpio a sex-crazed sadist. This book aims to paint a picture of what some of your choices might be and show what choices, conscious or unconscious, some well-known people of your sign have made.

Your upbringing will have helped shape what you believe about yourself and out of those beliefs comes, automatically, behaviour to match. For example, if you believe you are a victim, you will behave like one and the world will happily oblige by victimising you. If you see yourself as a carer, life will present you with plenty to care for – and often to care about, too. If you identify yourself as an adventurer, you'll spot opportunities at every corner. If you're a winner, then you'll tend to succeed. Shift the way that you see yourself and your whole world shifts, too.

Your Vocation

Your Sun describes your major life focus. This is not always a career. As the poet Milton said: 'They also serve who only stand and wait.' It is impossible to tell from your Sun sign exactly what your calling is – there are people of all signs occupied in practically every area of life. What is important is not so much *what* you do, but the way that you do it and it is this – how you express yourself – that your Sun describes. If you spend most of your time working at an occupation or living in a situation where you can't give expression to the qualities of your Sun, or which forces you to go against the grain of your Sun's natural inclinations, then you're likely to live a life of quiet, or possibly even noisy, desperation.

On Whose Authority

Your personality, which your birth chart maps, is like a sensitive instrument that will resonate only to certain frequencies – those that are similar to its own. Your Sun shows the kind of authority that will strike a chord with you, either positively or negatively, because it is in harmony with yours. It can show how you relate to people in authority, especially your father. (It is the Moon that usually shows the relationship with your mother and home.) In adult life it can throw light onto the types of bosses you are likely to come across, and also how you could react to them. It is a major part of the maturing process to take responsibility for expressing your own authority wisely. When you do so, many of your problems with external authorities diminish or even disappear.

In a woman's chart the Sun can also describe the kind of husband she chooses. This is partly because, traditionally, a husband had legal authority over his wife. It is also because, especially in the early years of a marriage, many women choose to pour their energies into homemaking and supporting their husbands' work in the world, rather than their own, and so his career becomes her career. As a

Piscean, you may find that your father, boss or husband shows either the positive or negative traits of Pisces or, as is usually the case, a mixture of both – compassionate, artistic and imaginative or passive, evasive and martyred.

Born on the Cusp

If you were born near the beginning or end of Pisces, you may know that your birthday falls on the cusp, or meeting point, of two signs. The Sun, however, can only be in one sign or the other. You can find out for sure which sign your Sun is in by checking the tables on pp. 98–99.

FOUR

The Drama of Being a Piscean

EACH SIGN IS ASSOCIATED WITH A CLUSTER OF ROLES THAT HAVE THEIR own core drama or story line. Being born is a bit like arriving in the middle of an ongoing play and slipping into a certain part. How we play our characters is powerfully shaped in early life by having to respond to the input of the other actors around us – the people that make up our families and communities. As the play of our lives unfolds, we usually become aware that there are themes which tend to repeat themselves. We may ask ourselves questions like 'Why do I always end up with all the work / caught up in fights / with partners who mistreat me / in dead-end jobs/ successful but unhappy . . .?' or whatever. Interestingly, I've found that people are less likely to question the wonderful things that happen to them again and again.

The good news is that once we recognise the way we have been playing our roles, we can then use our free-will choice to do some creative re-scripting, using the same character in more constructive scenarios. Even better news is that if we change, the other people in our dramas have got to make some alterations, too. If you refuse to respond to the same old cues in the customary ways, they are going to have to get creative, too.

A core role of Pisces is the dreamer. The words of the poet Arthur William Edgar O'Shaughnessy, himself a Piscean, sum up your sign beautifully:

> We are the music-makers,
> And we are the dreamers of dreams,
> Wandering by lone sea-breakers,
> And sitting by desolate streams;
> World-losers and world-forsakers,
> On whom the pale moon gleams:
> Yet we are the movers and shakers
> Of the world for ever, it seems.

One of the most famous dreamers in history was the ancient Chinese sage, Chuang Tzu. He dreamed that he was a butterfly, fluttering about, pleased with itself and happy, with no idea that Chuang Tzu existed. When he woke up, Chuang Tzu became himself again, but started to wonder whether it had been Chuang Tzu dreaming that he was a butterfly, or whether he was now a butterfly dreaming that it was Tzu. In dreams, reality is distorted and in vivid dreams the action seems very real indeed – often more so than that of waking reality. As a Piscean, you can flow easily between everyday reality and dream reality, and may sometimes be confused about which reality is true. Everything is relative, depending on the way you look at it.

In dreams there is also a sense of being both an onlooker and a participant at the same time. You are conscious and yet asleep, active and yet passive. Nothing is real and yet everything is real – in its own way. You can walk through walls and defy the laws of nature, and the fact that dream figures shift shape constantly seems both normal and natural. These figures can be recognisable or fantastical, yet they all have their own symbolic truth.

The land of dreams, which is your natural habitat, is a bit like the vast ocean that your ruler, Neptune, commands. It contains all that there is and its vistas and contents constantly change, distort and reveal. As a Piscean, the lure back into this kingdom, where all is potential and there are no separations, boundaries or responsibilities, is irresistible. The outside 'real' world can seem harsh, disappointing and painfully constricting compared to the exquisite beauty and endless possibilities of dreams. Some Pisceans escape as refugees into this magical land, safe from competition and adult responsibilities and remain, forever, unborn wraiths and passive passengers through the journey of life. But as the poet Yeats said, 'In dreams begins responsibility.' Not only is Pisces the last sign, it is also the first, and most Pisceans do learn to straddle both worlds, fulfilling their external obligations without abandoning their dreams. How you choose to see your role will determine your behaviour – are you a practical dreamer, using your access to the wisdom of the infinite to build a magnificent life, or do you prefer to remain a shadowy figure conjured up by someone else's reality?

Other Pisces roles are the medium, mystic, victim, martyr, rescuer, artist and poet.

The following chapter describes some typical Pisces behaviour. Remember, though, that there is no such thing as a person who is all Pisces and nothing but Pisces. You are much more complicated than that and other parts of your chart will modify, or may even seem to contradict, the single, but central, strand of your personality which is your Sun sign. These other sides of your nature will add colour and contrast and may restrict or reinforce your basic Pisces identity. They won't, however, cancel out the challenges you face as a Piscean.

FIVE

The Pisces Temperament

A SHIFTING SEA OF IMPRESSIONS FROM YOUR ENVIRONMENT washes through and around you, and being so impressionable, whether you are fully aware of it or not, every slight change in emotional tone registers in your body. It's as if you've been born porous, with very little protection against the world and its woes. You can walk into a room and pick up on the atmosphere instantly, especially if someone is upset or hurting. Their suffering, distress and vulnerability disturbs you and makes you feel vaguely guilty, so it can galvanise you into action to try to make it all better. Your heart bleeds for any person or creature that life has wounded or discarded. You're apt to notice, too, those that others overlook and walking past a shivering, unwashed beggar or an animal in need is often more than you can bear to do. With your boundless compassion, your tears come easily and you're always there when a helping hand is needed, scattering around countless little random acts of kindness, and many large ones, too.

No Boundary

Because of your acute sensitivity, you often experience other people's emotions as if they were your own. This is what gives you the precious gift of empathy – the ability to feel what it is like to be in another's situation – and the willingness to reach out to help. Sometimes, though, it's hard for you even to recognise that what you are feeling has nothing to do with you personally. You may be simply absorbing, and acting out, the feelings of those around you. When you learn to distinguish what is, and is not, yours and therefore what is, and is not, your responsibility to deal with, you are freed up from inappropriate entanglements and being sucked – and suckered – into other people's agendas.

Healing Presence

Nothing that people are capable of, no matter how vile, surprises you. Your attitude is 'There but for the grace of God go I' and, as you see right past these flaws and failings to connect with their essential humanness, you are moved to pity. Being able to accept another exactly the way they are, without judgement, is another name for love. Through this, you can help others accept themselves, too, so your presence alone can be healing. Others sense your openness, and you may find complete strangers unburdening themselves on you on trains and planes, as if you had a neon sign glowing on your forehead announcing 'Dump Your Troubles Here'.

No Way to Behave

Sometimes, though, a non-judgemental attitude can amount to a gross lack of judgement. By your acceptance, you could end up excusing or condoning anti-social or destructive behaviour. There's such a thing as idiot compassion. Because you often find it difficult to refuse a plea for assistance, people can see you as a soft touch and take you for a ride. Even if you've been let down repeatedly, you'll usually keep on trying to help. By indulging irresponsible behaviour and giving endless 'last chances', you're actually standing in the way of some people ever mending their ways and taking responsibility for their own lives. Painful though it may be, sometimes the most caring response is to say 'No!' very firmly – and mean it.

Conflict Cop-Out

You've a horror of confrontation and you'll do everything in your power to avoid it. You'd often rather put up with the most appalling conditions, suffering in silence or airbrushing it out of your mind, pretending that it isn't really happening, than tackle the situation directly. You can even be overly polite and utterly charming to people you detest. The root of all this evasion is your need to fuse with someone or something else. (Remember there are two fishes, not just one.) Emotional rapport is your life-blood and your whole identity is bound up with this sense of connectedness. Without it, you feel flawed and incomplete. Your dependence on 'the other' – whether this is a person, animal, organisation or ideal – is so great that any move towards independence or separation, on your part or the other's, can feel like a threat to your very existence. So you'll take care not to give offence in case your life-support system withdraws and you'll be abandoned into oblivion – something that, quite literally, you fear more than death.

Indirect Means

Your difficulty with saying 'No' means you often end up doing things you really don't want to do, trading on the hope that others will be equally selfless towards you. Because of the fear of refusal, which for you equals rejection, you may be scared to be upfront about getting your normal human needs and desires satisfied. You may even feel that you only have a right to exist by helping others through service and sacrifice, in the mistaken belief that sticking up for yourself is selfish, emotionally dangerous and not very nice. Some Pisceans are not always clear that they actually do have the right to breathe – and to take up space – without helping others first.

Getting What You Want

Most people, however, find it easier than you to state directly what they want – and as they are not as telepathic either, they can't read your mind. Although you find it almost impossible to get your head round this fact, some people really are selfish, cruel and insensitive, so when the supportive responses you expect from those you have gone out of your way to help aren't automatically forthcoming, you can seethe with indignation and bitter resentment. Feeling helpless and hurt, you may then be tempted to resort to emotional manoeuvring, using your instinctive understanding of atmospheric pressure to try to get your own needs met. Going down this road, however, will lead to what you fear most – being rejected and avoided, as most people become exceedingly angry if they sense they are being manipulated through guilt, and unspoken expectations and obligations.

To Be or Not To Be

Shakespeare, in the words of his most complex hero, summed up the dilemma that most Pisceans will recognise: 'To be, or not to be: that is the question' wondered Hamlet, and went on to contemplate the various possibilities – to suffer misfortunes passively, to try to end his troubles by confronting them actively, or to evade the whole issue by escaping into another reality. For many Pisceans, the jury is still out as to whether you actually want to be a fully committed participant in the theatre of life. You'll always

31

insert an escape clause in your contract somewhere. The truth is that you want to be free both 'to be' and 'not to be' and you much prefer to respond to situations as they arise, rather than initiate them yourself.

Creating Contentment

Your challenge is to know that *your* physical, emotional, mental and spiritual needs matter just as much as those of other people and to take responsibility for stating them openly and honestly and to find ways of having them met. Ask and you'll sometimes receive – and sometimes you'll be refused. Although it can seem like it at the time, refusal and rejection are not the end of your world. Each and every step you take away from fear-filled dependence on the emotional support of others towards genuine interdependence takes real courage, more than any other sign could ever know. By doing so, you'll find that not only do you survive, you thrive.

Sacrifice and Service

It's often said that Pisceans must either serve or suffer, and some do both. Many Pisceans find themselves in restricting circumstances or tied to inescapable duties, while others have a strong inner drive to sacrifice their own pleasures in the service of something greater than themselves. Without some kind of focus or limiting structure, imposed outwardly or inwardly, Pisceans can become helpless drifters, tossed about like a cork upon a stormy sea. If you view sacrifice as having to give something up, you could see yourself as a victim, or martyr, and make your own life, and those of others, completely miserable. If, on the other hand, you think of sacrifice in its original meaning of 'to make sacred', you will experience a sense of freedom, joy and fulfilment. The altruistic sacrifice of some Pisceans is awe-inspiring, like the Antarctic explorer Captain Lawrence Oates, who was lamed by frostbite. As this could have hindered his colleagues' chances of survival, he deliberately sacrificed his own life by walking out into a blizzard saying that he was just going outside, and might be some time . . .

Active Imagination

Pisceans are born actors. You love slipping into, and trying on, different roles just for fun. You especially love creating an aura of elusive desirability. The French writer Anaïs Nin, a Piscean, wrote that there were at least two women in her – one who was desperate and bewildered and felt as if she was drowning and another who would, as if on a stage, present to the world a smile, eagerness, curiosity and enthusiasm, concealing her true emotions because they were weaknesses, helplessness and despair. Some Pisceans are embarrassed by their secret vice of telling little white lies, like giving a false name on the telephone or saying you were at the library when you were really at the supermarket. You may or may not have anything to hide – your imagination is simply getting a workout. There's part of you that, no matter how close you are to someone, you'll always keep private. If anybody tries to pin you down, prise out your secrets, or becomes emotionally heavy, you'll slither away quietly. If backed into a corner, you'll simply lie. Albert Einstein said that imagination is more important than knowledge, and also that the distinction between past, present and future is only an illusion, however persistent. For you, everything is relative and, like the White Queen in Lewis Carroll's *Through the Looking Glass*, you find it easy to believe six impossible things before breakfast.

Escape From Reality

It was Piscean Liza Minnelli who said that reality is something you rise above. You need to take frequent holidays from time, space and the nitty-gritty of everyday life. There are many routes into an altered state. Participating in the swaying, baying mass that is a football or rugby crowd is, for many Piscean men, an authentic holy communion. Music, drama, poetry and love can be doorways to heaven, while other escapist activities like computer games, drugs, alcohol and junk food are particularly dangerous for you. These may numb the pain of existence temporarily, but you're prone to addictions and taking everything to excess. It's hard for you to know when to call a halt and some Pisceans end up just opting out of life altogether.

Mundane Matters

Negotiating the details of humdrum reality is not always easy. Some Pisceans – of all genders – are impeccably groomed beauties, radiating an aura of glamour and grace. Others clearly have difficulties with basic body maintenance, their ties or bosoms carrying spattered souvenirs of countless mealtimes past. In the same way, Pisceans can either be jaw-droppingly irresponsible or impressively creative with money – and sometimes both. You could be impulsively extravagant, ignoring away the constraints of the bank balance, or even the overdraft. You'd probably empty your wallet for anyone in need with no thought for tomorrow, trusting that it will all work out somehow. Yet some of the richest people in history have been born under the sign of the fish, like the founders of the Gulbenkian and Rothschild family dynasties. The latter gambled his all on Britain winning against Napoleon and when he received news of victory at Waterloo, bought and sold stock which netted him over £1 million profit.

Acute Intuition

One of your greatest assets is your ability to tap in to the vast ocean of emotion whose currents, from past, present and future, swirl and flow around all of us constantly. It's easy for you to get confused by this barrage of subtle impressions impinging on you, but by gently disciplining yourself to tune in, and to learn to interpret them, you'll have a rich source of wisdom, permanently on tap, to guide and protect you. Paying attention to your dreams and premonitions can help solve problems in the outer world and give you a strong competitive edge, as you can sense what vast numbers of people long for – and provide it. Some cater for the lowest common denominator, as media mogul Rupert Murdoch has been accused of doing, and make a fortune. Others, like Einstein and Galileo, shift world consciousness in higher ways.

Pisces at Work

Pisceans, like fish, come in all shapes and sizes – and with as many motivations. There are devilfish and angelfish and sharks and minnows, flounders and flukes, piranhas and suckers. What they all share is that fish can sense the way the current is flowing and adjust themselves to suit – and that is usually the path of least resistance.

Unless other chart factors indicate it, you're unlikely to be driven hard by worldly ambition or to be a lone self-starter. Being so adaptable, you can turn your hand to just about anything, from entrepreneurial high-flying to the humblest of jobs, but could be just as happy living off the state. Whether you're an aimless drifter or a practical dreamer depends on your external circumstances and what gods you serve. Working alone is rarely for you, as you need others around for support and structure. As an employer, you can be astute at instinctively picking the right person for the job. This ensures that you're surrounded by competent employees who can run the show responsibly with the minimum of effort from you. Because you hate confrontation, you also hate firing anyone, but you'll no doubt have a Capricorn or an Aries around to do any dirty work that's required.

The Caring Professions

Careers where your compassion, wisdom and insight into human nature are called for – like counselling, medicine, nursing or healing – are all excellent choices. Many Pisceans can be found in social-work departments, charities and churches. Working in prisons or psychiatric hospitals, or caring for animals or people with physical or mental disabilities, frequently in conditions that others would find intolerable, could suit you well.

Some of the greatest poets, artists, photographers, musicians and writers have been Pisceans, like Michelangelo, Renoir, Ansel Adams, Ravel and Chopin.

You have an uncanny sense of what people are just beginning to long for, which makes you a natural for working in the media, publishing and advertising, or in the worlds of theatre and film. Clients of Pisces hairdressers often leave the salon having had a therapy session as well as a cut and blow-dry. Because you love to be where the worldly and unworldly, real and imaginary, can merge and intermingle, you could feel at home in the world of spirits, literally or metaphorically. Many Pisceans are excellent ministers, clairvoyants and mystics, as well as wine merchants and pub-owners.

Pisces in Power

Surprisingly for a sign that can often seem so passive, many Pisceans hold powerful roles in business and politics, often working behind the scenes, secretly manipulating the show. You can be at the nerve centre of an operation, tuning in to what's going on around you, ducking out of the firing line until conditions are right, then taking advantage of opportunities and moving in for the prize. The temptation to cheat and take all, without responsibility or consequences, is great in Pisces, but be sure your sins will find you out.

Pisces and Health

As you tend to absorb other people's negativity, which sticks to you like grime, it's vital that you live and work in congenial surroundings, as emotional or physical pollution at work can make you unproductive or ill. You need to retreat from the world periodically and to be alone, preferably somewhere beautiful, silent and restful. This will allow you to shed psychic contamination and recharge your batteries. Without this, you're in danger of burning out. Learning to say 'no' when appropriate – and gritting your teeth to bear your almost inevitable guilt – is one of the best health investments you can make, as your tendency to rush to the rescue can leach away your energy and leave you feeling constantly drained. Your vitality can fluctuate wildly and is almost always dependent on your emotional state. Pisces is not a robust sign, but it is a resilient one. You may have many minor complaints but bounce back quickly with rest and a goodly helping of TLC. More than any other sign, you are prone to developing psychosomatic symptoms when something is troubling you, and you are either only vaguely aware of it or are trying to evade the issue. The body often talks in outrageously blatant puns, and once you have 'got it', accept the message and act on it and the problem can disappear remarkably quickly.

Feet on the Ground

Traditionally, Pisces rules the feet and walking barefoot can be beneficial, especially on unpolluted grassland, as not only do you pick up the Earth's subtle vibrations but you also discharge tensions with every step. Pisces also rules the lymphatics and the pineal gland, which produces chemicals responsible for sleeping, waking and altered states of consciousness – like dreaming. Typical ailments are allergies, chronic low-grade infections, frequent colds and flu, autoimmune diseases, addictions and foot problems. Many Pisceans forget to take good care of themselves and, as your sign is not famed for self-control, it's easy for you to indulge your appetites to excess, which can lead to liver and digestive problems and a tendency to retain water and gain weight. You may need to be particularly careful with alcohol because your body can be terribly sensitive to it, but, unfortunately, many born under the sign of the fish drink like one, too.

Pisces Relating

Being an incurable romantic, you're prone to delicious passing crushes and are almost always a little infatuated with somebody, frequently unobtainable. Your dream relationship is one where two hearts beat as one, with no need for words, and you never, ever again need feel alone or separate. Your fantasy is that love should be perfect, and everyone kind, gentle and endlessly supportive. Anything that jolts this vision of paradise comes as a very nasty shock. Because you go into relationships with such high expectations, it's easy to become disillusioned when everything turns out to be less than rosy. Accepting that unruffled bliss and happy-ever-afters only happen in fairy tales can improve your relationships enormously.

Pisces to the Rescue

You can be powerfully attracted to those in need of rescuing – people who are vulnerable, trapped or weak, or disabled though illness, addiction or emotional immaturity – or you may long to be rescued yourself. Relationships like this can bring out your loveliest qualities of tenderness and devotion and lead to long-lasting happiness. However, if you can only relate from the position of carer or cared-for, you could become overly dependent and find it hard to function on your own. If you, or your partner, then starts to recover, your abandonment terrors could be activated and you may be tempted to subtly sabotage the healing process to keep the relationship stable. There's no need to fall into this unhealthy pattern. Ideally, you and your partner could take turns to help and heal the other, deepening the relationship as you both grow stronger.

Pisces in Bed

Unless Aries or Scorpio figures strongly in your chart, anger and edgy hostility are complete turn-offs. Tenderness and gentle sensuality appeal more to you than rampant physical passion. What is important is that you feel wanted, and are often perfectly content to act out your erotic adventures, disembodied, in your imagination. With your intense sensitivity to moods and atmospheres, you like to set the scene with soft music, subtle scents and romantic candlelight. A glass or two of your favourite tipple shifts you into the pleasure of blurred-edge focus, for too much reality can spoil the moment. You may prefer your partner to take the initiative, and the dominant role, as surrender excites you and you love to be seduced.

Loving and Giving

Very little makes you jealous and you can forgive and forget just about anything, sometimes to a degree that borders on masochism. Your partner, however, may not be made of such noble stuff and your tendency not to cut the ties completely with former partners can be hard to bear. While you are usually loyal – technically at least, if not in your imagination – if things are less than loving at home, and the situation just happens to present itself, you could be tempted to stray. You would rarely, however, go out of your way to initiate an affair. Nor would you even think of leaving a relationship unless there's another one ready and waiting to step into, even if your present set-up is destructive and bitter. You can be a wonderful, tender lover, but harshness, coldness or disrespect for your dreams will make you withdraw and close down. You may stay present physically, but your spirit is elsewhere. Impotence and passive resistance are two of Pisces men's favourite weapons of war, while Pisces women turn elsewhere for emotional comfort – as often to caring work, romantic fiction or Mother Church as to the arms of another.

The Right Temperature

Just as water takes on the shape and qualities of whatever contains and surrounds it, you are responsive to those you associate with. It's essential, then, that you take care whom you allow into your intimate space, because you're wide open to their influence. Cold partners can chill you into misery while hot, temperamental ones could thoroughly destabilise you. You flourish in a haven of tenderness and support and are adept at creating a cosy cocoon for those you love.

SIX

Aspects of the Sun

PLANETS, JUST LIKE PEOPLE, CAN HAVE IMPORTANT RELATIONSHIPS WITH EACH other. These relationships are called aspects. Aspects to your Sun from any other planet can influence your personality markedly. The most powerful effects come with those from the slower-moving planets – Saturn, Uranus, Neptune or Pluto. Sometimes they can alter your ideas about yourself and your behaviour patterns so much that you may not feel at all typical of your sign in certain areas of your life.

Check if your birth date and year appear in the various sections below to find out if one or more of these planets was aspecting the Sun when you were born. Only the so-called challenging aspects have been included. These are formed when the planets are together, opposite or at right angles to each other in the sky.

Unfortunately, because space is restricted, other aspects have been left out, although they have similar effects to those described below and, for the same reason, a few dates will inevitably have been missed out, too. (You can find out for sure whether or not your Sun is aspected at my website www.janeridderpatrick.com.) If your Sun has no aspects to

Saturn, Uranus, Neptune or Pluto you're more likely to be a typical Pisces.

Some well-known Pisceans with challenging aspects to their Suns appear below. You can find more in the birthday section at the end of the book.

Sun in Pisces in Aspect with Saturn

Even if your birthday is not included below, if you were born between 1935 and 1937, 1964 and 1966 or 1994 and 1996, you are likely to feel the effect of Saturn on your Sun.

18–29 February in: 1935, 1943, 1949, 1956, 1963–4, 1972, 1979, 1985–6 and 1994

1–10 March in: 1936, 1943–4, 1950, 1957, 1965–6, 1973, 1978–80, 1986–7 and 1995

11–21 March in: 1937, 1944, 1951, 1958, 1966–7, 1974, 1980, 1987–8 and 1996

Sir Ranulph Fiennes	Calouste Gulbenkian	Kiri Te Kanawa
Baron Rothschild	Arthur Schopenhauer	Sharon Stone

It's important to find a way of making your mark on the world, while honouring too your urge to escape from it. You could be tempted to retreat into helplessness and passivity in the face of challenge, and so run the risk of becoming depressed and unfulfilled, as did the misery-guts philosopher of pessimism, Arthur Schopenhauer. He withdrew to live a bitter, reclusive life when he didn't receive the acknowledgement he felt he deserved. Or you could abandon your dreams, become cynical and live an outwardly successful but inwardly hollow life. The most difficult, but satisfying, solution is to stand by your dreams, then apply your steady determination to making them come true in the material world – like Sir Ranulph Fiennes, said to be the world's greatest living explorer. He has broken ten world records for polar and desert exploration and had his achievements crowned by honours from royalty and learned institutions. His outstanding physical and mental endurance is legendary – and every one of his expeditions is designed to make money for charity, over £4 million to date.

Your father may have been a disappointing or disappointed man, or have had strict expectations of you. Though tough, this can be turned to your advantage, fuelling a powerful ambition to become a recognised and respected pillar of whatever establishment you aspire to. The first Baron Rothschild and Calouste Gulbenkian both rose from humble origins and built vast fortunes from financial dealings with governments. Both founded powerful family dynasties, which have donated millions to help the underprivileged and to support the arts. You may not aspire to becoming a millionaire philanthropist, but you can create your own quiet empire of canniness and caring in your own backyard, and make a valued contribution to society at the same time.

Sun in Pisces in Aspect with Uranus

Even if your birthday is not included below, if you were born between 1962 and 1969, you are likely to feel the effect of Saturn on your Sun.

18–29 February in: 1943–6, 1962–5 and 1981–4
1–10 March in: 1945–8, 1964–7 and 1983–6
11–21 March in: 1948–50, 1967–9 and 1986–8

| Pam Ayers | Robin Cook | Galileo Galilei |
| Jerry Lewis | Liza Minnelli | George Washington |

One thing is sure. There is something about you that is different and doesn't conform to the standard for a Piscean

– or for anyone else, for that matter. No way will you, or even can you, fit into a box of anyone else's making. You may even enjoy shaking up and shocking the more entrenched attitudes of traditionalists, as you're a rebel and an innovator. Uranus, the planet of progress and reform, gives you an almost irresistible inclination to challenge and change the way things are. George Washington was Commander in Chief of the American army in the successful Revolutionary War against British rule and then became the first US president. At best, you have a crystal-clear view of what is outdated or unfair in a system and have original, and often controversial, ideas of how to bring about improvements.

At worst, you can be thought a bit of an oddball or just plain contrary. You may have an attitude problem around tradition and authority, which, of course, could provoke an almost inevitable backlash. Chances are, though, that many of your ideas that seem strange and unacceptable today will be mainstream a few years down the line. Take the great scientist and inventor Galileo. He was tried and imprisoned by the Church Inquisition for daring to provide proof to back up the outrageous and blasphemous theory that the Earth moves round the Sun.

Working with a group of like-minded people on innovative projects, making the world a better place for those who are suffering or are in some way disadvantaged could suit you well. You need frequent fresh challenges, as you easily become bored. Be careful, though, not to sabotage your own achievements through restlessness and by abruptly moving on when you start to become successful.

Sun in Pisces in Aspect with Neptune
18–29 February in: 1930–34 and 1969–75
1–10 March in: 1933–9 and 1974–80
11–21 March in: 1938–43 and 1979–84

| Kurt Cobain | Cindy Crawford | Ralph Nader |
| Boris Pasternak | Elizabeth Taylor | Joanne Woodward |

Boris Pasternak's epic romantic tragedy, *Doctor Zhivago*, captures the suffering of millions through the lens of one man's life. Sometimes it can feel as if the woes of the world have landed on you – and you'll feel miserable until you've tried to heal them. Your difficulty with saying 'no' to the emotional vampires who take advantage of your compassionate heart can be a major drain on your energy. Neptune heightens your sensitivity to other people's fantasies and longings. This can make you a natural for working in beauty, film, advertising and fashion, as you easily tap in to the field of dreams. The arts and the caring professions could suit you, too.

It's hard to pin you down, either physically or emotionally. Things are never quite what they seem when Neptune is involved. Others may see you as a victim or saviour, or some kind of icon. You may have idealised your father or found that he was emotionally unavailable for you in some way. You'll have had times of feeling vaguely guilty, inadequate and worthless for not being perfect and would much prefer to escape into your daydreams rather than face the harsh and limiting world outside. It's easy to become dependent on others to shore up your confidence. Some, like Elizabeth Taylor and Kurt Cobain, though seeming to have the world at their feet, are tempted to escape into the mists of mind-altering substances. This is best avoided, as you are highly susceptible to addictions.

At core, this is a spiritual aspect and your challenge is to find a way of losing yourself in serving something greater than your own ego. Joy comes through pouring your whole heart into your calling, whatever this is – caring for others, creating a happy home, protecting the environment or living for your art.

Sun in Pisces in Aspect with Pluto

18–29 February in: 1956–63 and 1994–2000
1–10 March in: 1962–8
11–21 March in: 1967–72

| Juliette Binoche | Sir Richard Burton | Patty Hearst |
| Steve Jobs | Josef Mengele | Michelangelo |

Pluto, like Scorpio, the sign it rules, runs to extremes. Power will come into your life in one form or another. Either you will be the one wielding it or you may have to grapple with the experience of being in the grip of a power greater than yourself in the form of money, sex, death, secrets, political might – or your own overwhelming compulsions. You can be a force for transforming the world around you, for good or ill. At one end of the spectrum there is Michelangelo, who, although he protested he was a sculptor, was forced by the pope to paint the ceiling of the Sistine Chapel, and after four long years of almost superhuman effort, produced one of the world's greatest masterpieces. At the other extreme is Josef Mengele, the Nazi doctor known as the 'Angel of Death', who was responsible for the torture and butchery of nearly half a million Jews in Auschwitz concentration camp. What unites these two is powerful ideals – in Michelangelo of art and religious devotion, and in Mengele an insane obsession with racial purity. Whatever ideals drive you, you have the determination and staying power to follow them through with intensity and persistence against the odds.

Sex and death may fascinate you. Or you may be drawn to poke into hidden, or even taboo, places that other people wouldn't venture – like the Victorian explorer Sir Richard Burton, who penetrated Mecca in disguise, found the source of the River Nile and translated the erotic classic, *The Kama Sutra*. You may go through some major life shifts, in which you'll have to leave the past behind and reinvent yourself. Trust the process and this becomes a cause for celebration and not for barricading yourself in against change.

SEVEN

Meeting Your Moon

☽ THE GLYPH FOR THE MOON IS THE SEMI-CIRCLE OR CRESCENT. It is a symbol for the receptiveness of the soul and is associated with feminine energies and the ebb and flow of the rhythms of life. In some Islamic traditions it represents the gateway to paradise and the realms of bliss.

The Sun and Moon are the two complementary poles of your personality, like yang and yin, masculine and feminine, active and reflective, career and home, father and mother. The Moon comes into its own as a guide at night, the time of sleeping consciousness. It also has a powerful effect on the waters of the earth. Likewise, the Moon in your birth chart describes what you respond to instinctively and feel 'in your waters', often just below the level of consciousness. It is your private radar system, sending you messages via your body responses and feelings, telling you whether a situation seems safe or scary, nice or nasty. Feelings provide vital information about circumstances in and around you. Ignore them at your peril; that will lead you into emotional, and sometimes even physical, danger. Eating disorders tend to be associated with being out of touch with, or neglecting, the instincts and the body, both of which the Moon describes.

Extraordinary though it might seem to those who are emotionally tuned in, some people have great difficulty in knowing what they are feeling. One simple way is to pay attention to your body. Notice any sensations that attract your attention. Those are linked to your feelings. Now get a sense of whether they are pleasant or unpleasant, then try to put a more exact name to what those feelings might be. Is it sadness, happiness, fear? What is it that they are trying to tell you? Your Moon hints at what will strongly activate your feelings. Learning to trust and decode this information will help make the world seem – and be – a safer place.

The Moon represents your drive to nurture and protect yourself and others. Its sign, house and aspects describe how you respond and adapt emotionally to situations and what feeds you, in every sense of the word. It gives information about your home and home life and how you experienced your mother, family and childhood, as well as describing your comfort zone of what feels familiar – the words 'family' and 'familiar' come from the same source. It shows, too, what makes you feel secure and what could comfort you when you're feeling anxious. Your Moon describes what moves and motivates you powerfully at the deepest instinctual level and indicates what is truly the 'matter' in – or with – your life.

Knowing children's Moon signs can help parents and teachers better understand their insecurities and respect their emotional make-up and needs, and so prevent unnecessary hurt, or even harm, to sensitive young lives. It's all too easy to expect that our children and parents should have the same emotional wiring as we do, but that's rarely how life works. Finding our parents' Moon signs can be a real revelation. It can often help us understand where they are coming from, what they need and why they react to us in the way they do. Many of my clients have been able to find the understanding and compassion to forgive their parents when they realised that they were doing their very best with the emotional resources available to them.

In relationships it is important that your Moon's requirements are met to a good enough extent. For example, if you have your Moon in Sagittarius you must have adventure, freedom and the opportunity to express your beliefs. If being with your partner constantly violates these basic needs, you will never feel secure and loved and the relationship could, in the long term, undermine you. However, if your Moon feels too comfortable, you will never change and grow. The art is to get a good working balance between support and challenge.

A man's Moon sign can show some of the qualities he will unconsciously select in a wife or partner. Some of the others are shown in his Venus sign. Many women can seem much more like their Moon signs than their Sun signs, especially if they are involved in mothering a family and being a support system for their husbands or partners. It is only at the mid-life crisis that many women start to identify more with the qualities of their own Suns rather than living that out through their partners' ambitions. Similarly, men tend to live out the characteristics of their Moon signs through their wives and partners until mid-life, often quite cut off from their own feelings and emotional responses. If a man doesn't seem at all like his Moon sign, then check out the women in his life. There's a good chance that his wife, mother or daughter will show these qualities.

Your Moon can be in any sign, including the same one as your Sun. Each sign belongs to one of the four elements: Fire, Earth, Air or Water. The element of your Moon can give you a general idea of how you respond to new situations and what you need to feel safe and comforted. We all become anxious if our Moon's needs are not being recognised and attended to. We then, automatically, go into our personal little rituals for making ourselves feel better. Whenever you are feeling distressed, especially when you are way out of your comfort zone in an unfamiliar situation, do something to feed and soothe your Moon. You're almost certain to calm down quickly.

Fire Moons

If you have a fire Moon in Aries, Leo or Sagittarius, your first response to any situation is to investigate in your imagination the possibilities for drama, excitement and self-expression. Feeling trapped by dreary routine in an ordinary humdrum life crushes you completely. Knowing that you are carrying out a special mission feeds your soul. To you, all the world's a stage and a voyage of discovery. Unless you are at the centre of the action playing some meaningful role, anxiety and depression can set in. To feel secure, you have to have an appropriate outlet for expressing your spontaneity, honourable instincts and passionate need to be of unique significance. The acknowledgement, appreciation and feedback of people around you are essential, or you don't feel real. Not to be seen and appreciated, or to be overlooked, can feel like a threat to your very existence.

Earth Moons

If you have an earth Moon in Taurus, Virgo or Capricorn, you'll respond to new situations cautiously and practically. Rapidly changing circumstances where you feel swept along and out of control are hard for you to cope with. You need time for impressions to sink in. Sometimes it is only much later, after an event has taken place, that you become sure what you felt about it. Your security lies in slowing down, following familiar routines and rituals, even if they are a bit obsessive, and focusing on something, preferably material – possibly the body itself or nature – which is comforting because it is still there. Indulging the senses in some way often helps too, through food, sex or body care. So does taking charge of the practicalities of the immediate situation, even if this is only mixing the drinks or passing out clipboards. To feel secure, you need continuity and a sense that you have your hand on the rudder of your own life. Think of the rather irreverent joke about the man seeming to cross himself in a crisis, all the while actually touching his most valued possessions to check that they are still intact – spectacles, testicles, wallet and watch. That must have been thought up by someone with the Moon in an earth sign.

Air Moons

When your Moon is in an air sign – Gemini, Libra or Aquarius – you feel most secure when you can stand back from situations and observe them from a distance. Too much intimacy chokes you and you'll tend to escape it by going into your head to the safety of ideas and analysis. Even in close relationships you need your mental, and preferably physical, space. You often have to think, talk or write about what you are feeling before you are sure what your feelings are. By putting them 'out there' so that you can examine them clearly, you can claim them as your own. Unfairness and unethical behaviour can upset you badly and make you feel uneasy until you have done something about it or responded in some way. It can be easy with an air Moon to be unaware of, or to ignore, your own feelings because you are more responsive to ideas, people and situations outside of yourself that may seem to have little connection with you. This is not a good idea, as it cuts you off from the needs of your body as well as your own emotional intelligence. Making opportunities to talk, play with and exchange ideas and information can reduce the stress levels if anxiety strikes.

Water Moons

Finally, if your Moon is in a water sign – Cancer, Scorpio or Pisces – you are ultra-sensitive to atmospheres, and you can experience other people's pain or distress as if they were your own. You tend to take everything personally and, even if the situation has nothing at all to do with you, feel responsible for making it better. Your worst nightmare is to feel no emotional response coming back from other people. That activates your deep-seated terror of abandonment, which can make you feel that you don't exist and is, quite literally, what you fear even more than death. If you feel insecure, you may be tempted to resort to emotional manipulation to try to force intimacy with others – not a good idea, as this can lead to the very rejection that you dread. You are at your most secure when the emotional climate is positive and you have trusted, supportive folk around who will winkle you out of hiding if you become too reclusive. With a water Moon, it is vital to learn to value your own feelings and to take them seriously – and to have a safe, private place you can retreat to when you feel emotionally fragile. As you never forget anything which has made a feeling impression on you, sometimes your reactions are triggered by unconscious memories of things long past, rather than what is taking place in the present. When you learn to interpret them correctly, your feelings are your finest ally and will serve you well.

Finding Your Moon Sign

If you don't yet know your Moon sign, before looking it up, you could have some fun reading through the descriptions that follow and seeing if you can guess which one it is. To find your Moon sign, check your year and date of birth in the tables on pp. 100–113. For a greater in-depth understanding of your Moon sign, you might like to read about its characteristics in the book in this series about that sign.

At the beginning of each section are the names of some well-known Pisceans with that particular Moon sign. You can find more about them in Chapter Ten.

Sun in Pisces with Moon in Aries

Galileo Galilei	Jean Harlow	Yitzhak Rabin
James Redfield	Lynn Redgrave	James Taylor

Part of you thrives on risk, excitement and competition so you could often find yourself in situations of conflict. With your fiercely independent streak, you're determined to have your own way and hate being told what to do, yet you're also highly dependent on others for support. Action will colour your life, one way or another, but hopefully not a violently as in the case of Jean Harlow, the actress known as the Blonde Bombshell, who was beaten senseless by one husband and bullied, and effectively killed, through neglect, by her domineering mother. The challenge of this Moon is to learn to stick up for yourself courageously, without causing harm to yourself or others. There are ways of living risk safely – perhaps in your imagination, like James Redfield, who wrote the spiritual adventure parable *The Celestine Prophecy*, which became a runaway bestseller.

You could be excellent at pioneering or spearheading campaigns. You need a noble ideal to serve, one that is bigger than your own ego, and into which you can throw all of that passion and fiery energy, even if it does mean self-sacrifice. Yitzhak Rabin was the Israeli prime minister who won a Nobel Peace Prize for his part in the agreement of Israel to withdraw from disputed territories – and was later assassinated for his stance by an Israeli extremist. At home, you're likely, physically or emotionally, to put prolific amounts of energy into creating a secure, solid and comfortable base for yourself and your family. When under too much pressure and feeling guilty about saying 'no' or protecting your boundaries, you can develop splitting headaches. Strenuous physical exercise could be just the thing to restore you when the going gets tough.

Sun in Pisces with Moon in Taurus

Edgar Cayce	Neville Chamberlain	Christine Keeler
Ariel Sharon	Sandie Shaw	Julie Walters

You put a high value on stability and may, like British prime minister Neville Chamberlain, prefer peace at almost any price. Before the Second World War, he tried to appease Hitler, and having extracted a promise from the Führer not to go to war, claimed to have achieved 'peace with honour'. When Hitler broke his promise, he destroyed Chamberlain's reputation, too. However, as well as promoting peace, Chamberlain was also quietly stocking up on armaments. With hindsight, it might actually have been his delaying tactics that made eventual Allied victory possible. Similarly, the main aim in life for Israeli prime minister Ariel Sharon is to ensure total security for Israel – but this time on his terms. In your own way, like these two leaders, your combination of high ideals, dogged determination and down-to-earth practicality means that your focus is on peace and prosperity.

You love to feel solid earth beneath your feet. For singer Sandie Shaw, this was literal – she used to appear on stage barefoot. Security for you lies in having enough in the bank, your own roof over your head and a continuous supply of sensual pleasures. Art and music feed your soul and food, glorious food – and comforting sex – will always be of interest. You are a creature of habit and when events change too fast and you feel your control being swept away, you'll head straight back to the reassurance of these basics. Edgar Cayce was a trance medium whose channelled messages saved the lives and health of thousands yet, when he was ill himself, he refused to take the advice that came through for him about changing his lifestyle, preferring to stick to the familiar fry-ups and tobacco that hastened his end.

Sun in Pisces with Moon in Gemini

Lord Snowdon	W.H. Auden	Lady Isabel Burton
Adelle Davis	Lawrence Durrell	Harold Wilson

'Blessed be they who invented pens, ink, and paper!' – the words of Lady Isabel Burton, inveterate Victorian traveller and diarist. You might like to add phones and e-mails and faxes. Not being able to communicate your feelings and thoughts to paper, or to others, is for you like being starved of oxygen. It's often only in the process of expressing them in words that you discover what your feelings really are. Talking or writing about them can help heal any emotional wounds and dissolve accumulated resentments. Words and ideas fascinate you, and you love to play games with them. You can be a skilled illusionist, picking up the drift of what you think people want to hear and delivering the goods – a considerable advantage in politics and marketing. Former British prime minister Harold Wilson carefully cultivated his image as an ordinary, working-class lad from Yorkshire, with his props of pipe, HP sauce and raincoat. He was actually a highly educated scholar with an encyclopaedic memory, and a master of political tactics with a legendary reputation as an escapologist – and in private much preferred cigars to a pipe.

Despite your reclusive streak, you're unlikely to be a party pooper, as you like to be socially active and are skilled at flirting. With your low boredom threshold and powerful curiosity, you can be carried away by the distractions of the moment. Settling down in one place isn't always easy and there may be several places you could call home. Your restlessness, love of freedom and hunger for novelty mean you can't bear to be tied down to too much routine. Being constantly on the move like this keeps you young at heart.

Sun in Pisces with Moon in Cancer

| Drew Barrymore | Jilly Cooper | Neil Hamilton |
| Liza Minnelli | Vita Sackville-West | Kenneth Williams |

Moon in Cancer tends to divide the world up into 'us' and 'them', and it's crucial for your emotional comfort that you feel accepted by those you classify as 'us'. Sometimes your need to belong can come in odd disguises – like snobbery, ordinary or inverted. Vita Sackville-West, author, lesbian lover of Virginia Woolf and creator of one of Britain's most beautiful gardens at Sissinghurst Castle, looked down her long, aristocratic nose on the dreadful middle classes. Jilly Cooper's book, *Class*, is a wickedly insightful exposé of who excludes whom in the English class system. Being overly touchy, it's all too easy for you to take criticism, real or imagined, far too personally and then withdraw into sulky blame and resentment, mixed with tortured self-criticism – and sometimes into chemically induced blot-out. The hallmark of comedian Kenneth Williams, star of the popular *Carry On* films, was flared-nostril outrage at any perceived slight. Like so many with this combination, he was an acutely sensitive individual who hid behind acting to protect himself.

Safety and intimacy are essential for your well-being, and you may be more timid and dependent than you care to admit, even to yourself. Though you might appear the dominant one, you love being under the wing of a stronger personality, and without the safety net of emotional, financial and domestic security, you can become quite ungrounded. What is familiar is what feels safe. Family, or close friends and colleagues, are your chosen in-group with whom you can barricade yourself away from the potentially hostile world outside, but you are gentle, kind and helpful to anyone in need or distress. Your ability to pick up instinctively what the people long for can make you a natural for working with the public.

Sun in Pisces with Moon in Leo

Ansel Adams	Douglas Bader	Gordon Brown
Mikhail Gorbachev	Miranda Richardson	Ellen Terry

With your Moon in the regal sign of Leo, you hate to be overlooked. You're drawn to all that's finest and probably dress and present yourself beautifully. As you're a natural performer, it's important to find an appropriate outlet for your leadership skills – and desire to be in the limelight – perhaps through art or acting, or championing the underdog. Douglas Bader lost both legs at the age of 21 in a flying accident, yet through sheer willpower and heroism overcame his disability and went on to command an air squadron in the Battle of Britain. As a POW, he repeatedly tried to escape from Colditz Castle and after the war set up a charity for amputees. His belief was that a disabled person who fights back is not handicapped, but inspired. He could have added 'inspiring', as he indeed was, and you can be, too. You are able to walk with the great and good yet empathise with the humblest, like Russian leader Mikhail Gorbachev, who identified strongly with both the Russian workers and world leaders and helped to bring about the end of the Cold War.

The downside of this mix is caricatured by Miranda Richardson's character Queenie in *Blackadder*, who wants to chop off people's heads and show who is boss! If you were ignored and put down as a child, and weren't allowed to be spontaneous and sparkling, you may be hungry for attention and will try to hog the limelight, usually completely unconsciously. No matter how self-effacing you seem, if your dignity is ruffled you can become hurt or haughty, as you hate to be seen in a bad light. Fortunately, your preference is to act honourably, which will bring you the appreciation you need.

Sun in Pisces with Moon in Virgo

Douglas Adams   Nick Leeson   Luther Burbank
Jeanne Louise Calment Alexander Graham Rudolph Steiner
                              Bell

How things work – physical, emotional, mental or spiritual – fascinates you and you'll often enjoy linking this with your love of art, spirituality or caring for the disadvantaged. The legacy of social philosopher and mystic Rudolf Steiner lives on in a worldwide network of Waldorf Schools, as well as homes for the mentally and physically handicapped. These value the dignity of the individual and successfully combine beauty, spirituality and efficiency. With your inventive mind, eye for detail and keen intuition, you can find ways and means of fixing virtually anything – from practical problems to dodgy deals. Alexander Graham Bell's invention of the telephone came directly from his experience of using phonetics to help the deaf to speak, while rogue trader Nick Leeson brought down Barings Bank by using his talents to try to fiddle the financial markets – and almost succeeded.

Doing things well gives you a quiet sense of satisfaction, but you may have to resist the temptation to become a workaholic. On a bad day you can be hypersensitive, anxious and critical. If that happens, put your house in order – literally. There is nothing like sharpening your pencils and re-arranging your files to make the world feel a better place. You may have an interest in health and healing, but still be fond of comforting bad habits. Jeanne Louise Calment, who died in 1997 at the age of 122, was still exercising regularly and riding her bicycle at 100 – but only gave up smoking at 112! There is part of you that can hanker, nun- or monk-like, after the innocent purity of an ordered life. Simplicity suits you, so stripping down to essentials and de-junking your life could be a perfect tonic from time to time.

Sun in Pisces with Moon in Libra

Rudolph Nureyev	Nat 'King' Cole	Patty Hearst
Elizabeth Barrett Browning	Sidney Poitier	Karen Silkwood

A Libra Moon frequently means an interest in romance, or politics. An odd coupling you might think, but what links them is the love of correct relationship, since equality is the only basis for harmony and justice. You may be drawn to civil rights, like Nat 'King' Cole, the black singer with a voice like velvet. To be allowed to stay in the places where he sang, he successfully sued hotel chains that practised racial discrimination. Men with this combo are often willing to do their fair share of housework and childcare – without being nagged. Standing up for others gives you phenomenal courage. Karen Silkwood, concerned about health dangers to fellow workers at a nuclear power plant, collected evidence about leakages and falsified records, but died in suspicious circumstances before presenting the evidence.

Without a relationship you can feel incomplete, but it's all too easy for you to be drawn into other people's realities – even that of enemies. Patty Hearst, a publishing heiress, was kidnapped by a gang who extorted $6 million from her wealthy family, to feed the poor. She joined them in an armed bank robbery and was jailed herself. As you can find decision-making difficult, you'd often rather let others shoulder the responsibility of making your choices. Being idealistic to the point of naivety, and easily hurt and disappointed, you may prefer to stay aloof from everyday life. But just as eggs need to be broken to make an omelette, it's only by breaking out of your ivory tower that you can realise your potential. As beauty and harmony feed you, all disagreements are best settled quickly (but without compromising your principles) and, ideally, your home should be a haven of light and elegance.

Sun in Pisces with Moon in Scorpio

| Prince Andrew | Cyrano de Bergerac | John Leslie |
| John Steinbeck | Lytton Strachey | Elizabeth Taylor |

You have deep empathy with anyone or anything whose survival is at stake and will move in swiftly to care for and protect them. The subject of John Steinbeck's most famous book, *The Grapes of Wrath*, was poor people faced with disaster, crushing poverty and injustice, and its publication led to much-needed reforms. You make a rock-solid friend, but a formidable foe. If you feel betrayed, you may forgive – possibly – but never forget and you may retaliate even if you yourself get hurt in the process. French writer Cyrano de Bergerac was bullied because of his grotesque nose but, instead of putting up with being scapegoated, he retaliated and claimed to have fought more than a thousand duels over it.

Your feelings are intense and you can be fearless about tackling anything that stinks of vice, intimidation or hypocrisy. Lytton Strachey's biographical bombshell, *Eminent Victorians*, ruthlessly dished the dirt on those who had been previously seen in a smug and saintly light, like Florence Nightingale and General Gordon. As a child, you would have been acutely aware of undercurrents of power, sensing that there were certain subjects that were not to be talked about in your family or community. Those are the very forbidden areas that you could be magnetically drawn to – intentionally or not – like sex, death, wealth and trauma. As it is hard for you to trust, you tend to be secretive about your true feelings, revealing them only when you are absolutely sure of your confidant, or never at all. You have a deep reserve of emotional power that comes to your aid when your back is to the wall. You're a survivor and threat can bring out the best or the worst in you.

Sun in Pisces with Moon in Sagittarius

| Levi Strauss | Albert Einstein | Rupert Murdoch |
| Nicolaus Copernicus | Valentina Tereshkova | Ivana Trump |

Your instinct is, wherever possible, to push back the frontiers and expand your knowledge and experience, whether this is geographical, mental, spiritual, romantic or material. The bigger and further the better, as far as you are concerned and, when it comes to travelling, nothing comes much bigger or further than outer space. So it's fascinating, but unsurprising, that the first man and first woman in space, Yuri Gagarin and Valentina Tereshkova, both have this Sun–Moon combination. So had Nicolaus Copernicus, who shattered the medieval world-view with the theory that the Sun, and not the Earth, was the centre of the universe. Another boundary-expander was Albert Einstein, who transcended accepted theories on the nature of time by daydreaming of riding on a sunbeam, at the speed of light, to the end of the universe. This led directly to the development of nuclear energy.

Your uncanny ability to sense what the world wants next and to spot, and profit from, opportunities and gaps in the market means you have the Midas touch, provided you don't push your luck too far – which you're often tempted to do. Levi Strauss moved to California during the gold rush intending to supply miners with tents. Finding no market for those, he shifted gear and struck gold himself by using his stout canvas to make riveted 'waist overalls' – now better known as jeans. The fields of teaching, publishing and broadcasting could be highly profitable for you. Rupert Murdoch has expanded from owning one small newspaper in Adelaide to dominating a global media empire. You may also be attracted to sports – like Ivana Trump, who was a professional skier before she segued into over-the-top glamour. Knowing when to stop could be a major challenge for you . . .

Sun in Pisces with Moon in Capricorn

| Juliette Binoche | Robin Cook | Anaïs Nin |
| Samuel Pepys | Dinah Shore | George Washington |

Your habit of shouldering – or feeling crushed by – responsibilities has its roots in childhood, where you could have experienced deprivation, or frustrations, of some kind. Your parents may have been poor, elderly or unable to give you much in the way of emotional support. If material circumstances were comfortable, you could have been denied the freedom to be a spontaneous child and expected to behave according to other people's strict expectations. So you tend to feel that life is hard and love has to be earned.

Yet all of this gives you major advantages: you are well able to look after yourself and those you feel responsible for. The father of George Washington, the first US president, died young, leaving a large family and very little money. From boyhood, George, sober beyond his years, took on the responsibility for bringing up his extended family. He sensibly married a rich widow and went on to become one of the first US millionaires. He is described as rich in common sense, a good manager and a dignified, well-dressed gentleman. A perfect example of the Pisces–Capricorn mix, in fact.

Finding some long-term ambition to work towards slowly, but surely, could help you feel secure. Dinah Shore, crippled by polio at the age of two, through sheer grit went on to be the first woman with her own prime-time TV variety show. Approval and social recognition matter to you and you thrive when you find some responsible role in the community. Without one, you may feel lost or even depressed. Oddly, solitude and sinking into melancholy feed you, so it is important to allow yourself to indulge in them from time to time – and to enjoy the fruits of all your hard work, too.

Sun in Pisces with Moon in Aquarius

Glenn Close	Prince Edward	Sheila Hancock
Robin Knox-Johnston	Miriam Makeba	Joanne Woodward

There was probably something unusual, or disruptive, about your home life or childhood. Glenn Close shuttled between the Congo in Africa, where her doctor father ran a clinic, and exclusive boarding schools in Switzerland. Being walled into the confines of a small and cosy nuclear family is unlikely to have much appeal, as where you feel you truly belong is in the wider community. Friendship matters a great deal and friends can often feel like your real family. They may live at the far ends of the earth, and you might not see each other from one decade's end to the next, but for you, once a friend, always a friend and you're usually the first on the scene in case of need.

You could have an urge to live or work communally, or to improve the lives of those who are socially excluded or treated unfairly. Although you feel that you're just one of the crowd, at the same time you may often sense that you don't quite fit in. Your moods can be contrary. One moment you may be abrupt and withdrawn, then you'll be chatty and friendly the next. You may even neglect to feed, water and exercise your body unless you're prompted. Others may see you as aloof – and possibly even a bit of an oddball or loner – and often ahead of the crowd in your ideas and passions. In the 1960s, when apartheid split South Africa, Miriam Makeba was the first singer to put African music on the international map. As a human-rights campaigner, she was also the first of many black artists to go into voluntary exile in protest. Like her, social justice often matters more to you than your own personal comfort.

Sun in Pisces with Moon in Pisces

Cindy Crawford	James Goldsmith	Sharon Stone
Pat Nixon	Maurice Ravel	George Friedrich Handel

Being so sensitive and suggestible, you need to choose with care those you allow to become close to you. It's all too easy for you to be sucked into other people's realities and to lose your own direction. Especially dangerous for you are negative atmospheres, because you are wide open to psychic contamination. The positive side of this is that you are equally open to the enchantment of beauty and goodness and love. You've the gift, too, of tuning in to other people's thoughts and longings and giving them expression, which is invaluable if you are a performer, artist or designer, as you can effortlessly tap in to, and capture, the public imagination. Ravel's *Bolero* is reputed to be the most frequently played piece of music in the classical repertoire.

As you live so much in your imagination, you can truly create your own reality. Poetry and beauty are food for your soul but you may overlook orderly matters when it comes to home-making. Chaos, however, is frequently the essential first step towards creativity. You tend to shrink away from harshness of any kind and could prefer to be reclusive. Pat Nixon, wife of US president Richard Nixon, had to sacrifice her love of privacy for the sake of her husband's career. Escaping from everyday reality – and bouts of low self-esteem – is essential for your well-being. It's best if retreat doesn't come through alcohol or drugs, as you can get lost in fantasy or fear, deception or dependency – or even addiction. Your best qualities develop when you use your gifts to help rescue those that mainstream life has cast off – Handel's glorious musical poem of redemption, *Messiah*, was written for charity concerts in Dublin. Just refuse to be manipulated by guilt into spreading yourself too thinly.

EIGHT

Mercury – It's All in the Mind

THE GLYPHS FOR THE PLANETS ARE MADE UP OF THREE SYMBOLS: THE circle, the semi-circle and the cross. Mercury is the only planet, apart from Pluto, whose glyph is made up of all three of these symbols. At the bottom there is the cross, representing the material world; at the top is the semi-circle of the crescent Moon, symbolising the personal soul; and in the middle, linking these two, is the circle of eternity, expressed through the individual. In mythology, Mercury was the only god who had access to all three worlds – the underworld, the middle world of earth and the higher world of the gods. Mercury in your chart represents your ability, through your thoughts and words, to make connections between the inner world of your mind and emotions, the outer world of other people and events, and the higher world of intuition. Your Mercury sign can give you a great deal of information about the way your mind works and about your interests, communication skills and your preferred learning style.

It can be frustrating when we just can't get through to some people and it's easy to dismiss them as being either completely thick or deliberately obstructive. Chances are they are neither. It may be that you're simply not talking each other's languages. Knowing your own and other people's communication styles can lead to major breakthroughs in relationships.

Information about children's natural learning patterns can help us teach them more effectively. It's impossible to learn properly if the material isn't presented in a way that resonates with the way your mind works. You just can't 'hear' it, pick it up or grasp it. Wires then get crossed and the data simply isn't processed. Many children are seriously disadvantaged if learning materials and environments don't speak to them. You may even have been a child like that yourself. If so, you could easily have been left with the false impression that you are a poor learner just because you couldn't get a handle on the lessons being taught. Identifying your own learning style can be like finding the hidden key to the treasure room of knowledge.

The signs of the zodiac are divided into four groups by element:

> The fire signs: Aries, Leo and Sagittarius
> The earth signs: Taurus, Virgo and Capricorn
> The air signs: Gemini, Libra and Aquarius
> The water signs: Cancer, Scorpio and Pisces

Your Mercury will therefore belong to one of the four elements, depending on which sign it is in. Your Mercury can only be in one of three signs – the same sign as your Sun, the one before or the one after. This means that each sign has one learning style that is never natural to it. For Pisces, this is the earth style.

Mercury in each of the elements has a distinctive way of

operating. I've given the following names to the learning and communicating styles of Mercury through the elements. Mercury in fire – active imaginative; Mercury in earth – practical; Mercury in air – logical; and Mercury in water – impressionable.

Mercury in Fire: Active Imaginative

Your mind is wide open to the excitement of fresh ideas. It responds to action and to the creative possibilities of new situations. Drama, games and storytelling are excellent ways for you to learn. You love to have fun and play with ideas. Any material to be learned has to have some significance for you personally, or add to your self-esteem, otherwise you rapidly lose interest. You learn by acting out the new information, either physically or in your imagination. The most efficient way of succeeding in any goal is to make first a mental picture of your having achieved it. This is called mental rehearsal and is used by many top sportsmen and women as a technique to help improve their performance. You do this spontaneously, as your imagination is your greatest mental asset. You can run through future scenarios in your mind's eye and see, instantly, where a particular piece of information or situation could lead and spot possibilities that other people couldn't even begin to dream of. You are brilliant at coming up with flashes of inspiration for creative breakthroughs and crisis management.

Mercury in Earth: Practical

Endless presentations of feelings, theories and possibilities can make your eyes glaze over and your brain ache to shut down. What really turns you on is trying out these theories and possibilities to see if they work in practice. If they don't, you'll tend to classify them 'of no further interest'. Emotionally charged information is at best a puzzling nonstarter and at worst an irritating turn-off. Practical demonstrations, tried and tested facts and working models fascinate you. Hands-on learning, where you can see how a process functions from start to finish, especially if it leads to some useful material end-product, is right up your street. It's important to allow yourself plenty of time when you are learning, writing or thinking out what to say, otherwise you can feel rushed and out of control, never pleasant sensations for earth signs. Your special skill is in coming up with effective solutions to practical problems and in formulating long-range plans that bring concrete, measurable results.

Mercury in Air: Logical

You love learning about, and playing with, ideas, theories and principles. Often you do this best by arguing or bouncing ideas off other people, or by writing down your thoughts. Your special gift is in your ability to stand back and work out the patterns of relationship between people or things. You much prefer it when facts are presented to you logically and unemotionally and have very little time for the irrational, uncertainty or for personal opinions. You do, though, tend to have plenty of those kinds of views yourself, only you call them logical conclusions. Whether a fact is useful or not is less important than whether it fits into your mental map of how the world operates. If facts don't fit in, you'll either ignore them, find a way of making them fit, or, occasionally, make a grand leap to a new, upgraded theory. Yours is the mind of the scientist or chess player. You make a brilliant planner because you can be detached enough to take an overview of the entire situation.

Mercury in Water: Impressionable

Your mind is sensitive to atmospheres and emotional undertones and to the context in which information is presented. Plain facts and figures can often leave you cold and even intimidated. You can take things too personally and read between the lines for what you believe is really being said or taught. If you don't feel emotionally safe, you can be cautious about revealing your true thoughts. It may be hard, or even impossible, for you to learn properly in what you sense is a hostile environment. You are excellent at impression management. Like a skilful artist painting a picture, you can influence others to think what you'd like them to by using suggestive gestures or pauses and intonations. People with Mercury in water signs are often seriously disadvantaged by left-brain schooling methods that are too rigidly structured for them. You take in information best through pictures or images, so that you get a 'feel' for the material and can make an emotional bond with it, in the same way you connect with people. In emotionally supportive situations where there is a rapport between you and your instructors, or your learning material, you are able just to drink in and absorb circulating knowledge without conscious effort, sometimes not even being clear about how or why you know certain things.

Finding Your Mercury Sign

If you don't yet know your Mercury sign, you might like to see if you can guess what it is from the descriptions below before checking it out in the tables on pp. 114–15.

Sun in Pisces with Mercury in Aries

Michael Caine	Nat 'King' Cole	Albert Einstein
Liza Minnelli	Philip Roth	Sharon Stone

Though you may not always be aware of it, you have a mind like a weapon of war. In the heat of the moment, you can come out with some pretty aggressive and cutting remarks, ones that are usually best left unsaid and that can wound deeply. The more unconscious of your aggression you are, the more retaliation you'll attract from others. Using your incisive mental energy to slice to the heart of the matter, and to push back new frontiers, can bring immense benefits, both for yourself and for others. Albert Einstein ranks as one of the greatest pioneers in advancing our understanding of the universe. It takes courage to step out of the box to think and to say what few would ever risk. Philip Roth came into conflict with conservatives who tried to restrict access to his books, like *Portnoy's Complaint*, because they dared to deal with subjects which were, at the time, too risqué to be mentioned in polite company, like abortion and masturbation.

Your restless mind is constantly on the lookout for fresh and preferably stimulating ideas and information. Controversy, conflict and competition attract your attention. When bored, you just switch off and disappear into your active imagination. Life for you is not a spectator sport. You prefer ideas that are the mental equivalent of throwing down the gauntlet. Unlike most Pisceans, litigation and arguments rarely faze you – as long as you're the one attacking. Nat 'King' Cole was involved in many lawsuits, which he usually won. You can also be refreshingly open and upfront. Michael Caine honestly admits that he chooses which films to star in based on two criteria – where they will be shot, and how much money he will earn.

Sun in Pisces with Mercury in Aquarius

| Emile Coué | Adelle Davis | Michel de Montaigne |
| Patrick Moore | Willie Rodger | George Washington |

Your views are often unorthodox but you'll express them anyway, sometimes taking an almost perverse delight in startling or upsetting those on the receiving end. Your learning and communication style may even be quirky and original, too. Astronomer Patrick Moore has delighted TV audiences since the late 1950s with his mad-scientist enthusiasm and machine-gun delivery. Michel de Montaigne, France's equivalent of Shakespeare and inventor of the essay, was, as an experiment, only allowed to speak Latin until he was six years old.

Truth – as you see it – matters to you and you'll rarely let convention stand in the way. There may or may not be any truth in the story of the young George Washington owning up to having destroyed a precious cherry tree with 'I can't tell a lie, Pa; you know I can't tell a lie. I did cut it with my hatchet', but the principle is true for those with Mercury in Aquarius. Your truth can hurt, though, as at times your Piscean sensitivity and compassion can entirely desert you.

Once an idea has lodged in your mind it remains there, stubbornly embedded, despite all evidence to the contrary. You may pick up progressive new ideas that are just starting to circulate and become their mouthpiece. What you say, and how you say it, may seem shocking or weird today, but tomorrow could be taken for granted as plain common sense. Emile Coué, the pioneer of autosuggestion, now an increasingly accepted self-help tool, aroused both controversy and interest with his phrase 'Every day, in every way, I am becoming better and better.' The breath-taking clarity and logic of your flashes of inspiration seem to come from a higher realm altogether – perhaps they do.

Sun in Pisces with Mercury in Pisces

L. Ron Hubbard	Edgar Cayce	Lawrence Durrell
Elizabeth Barrett Browning	Nina Simone	Rudolph Steiner

As your mind is so impressionable to subtle nuances, you learn best through poetry, images and music, and by just soaking up atmospheres. With your free-floating imagination, you can seem dreamy and absent-minded, but are also highly creative. Traditional teaching methods don't always work in your favour, as you are a right-brain learner – much better at non-verbal communication than logic. You can tune in to the vast, diffuse and shifting ocean of invisible mental and emotional material that all life is immersed in, and pluck out pearls. But as it can be hard for you to articulate your inner experiences in words, you may not always be understood. Lawrence Durrell's school report said that he was a mine of disinformation. Being a natural intuitive, it can take you a great deal of time and experience to learn to distinguish your own thoughts and feelings from those that are coming from people around you. This kind of sensitivity has its advantages: Edgar Cayce was one of the finest, and best documented, psychics ever. Some of his channelled advice about medicines included those that would only be invented many years later.

Being both mentally and emotionally responsive, take

care that you don't get tangled up in emotional manipulation and become needlessly guilty, then resentful. You are often inconsistent, you'll say one thing today and another tomorrow and both will be true – at the time you said them. For you, everything is relative – you don't believe in absolutes. While this can make you tolerant, it can also lead to woolly thinking and confusion. You can be skilled at conveying vivid verbal impressions of what you sense people want to hear, rather than always telling the precise, literal truth. Children with this combination often need to be taught, gently but firmly, the difference between fact and fiction.

NINE

Venus – At Your Pleasure

♀ THE GLYPH FOR VENUS IS MADE UP OF THE CIRCLE OF ETERNITY on top of the cross of matter. Esoterically this represents love, which is a quality of the divine, revealed on earth through personal choice. The saying 'One man's meat is another man's poison' couldn't be more relevant when it comes to what we love. It is a mystery why we find one thing attractive and another unattractive, or even repulsive. Looking at the sign, aspects and house of your Venus can't give any explanation of this mystery, but it can give some clear indications of what it is that you value and find desirable. This can be quite different from what current fashion tells you you should like. For example, many people are strongly turned on by voluptuous bodies but the media constantly shows images of near-anorexics as the desirable ideal. If you ignore what you, personally, find beautiful and try to be, or to love, what at heart leaves you cold, you are setting yourself up for unnecessary pain and dissatisfaction. Being true to your Venus sign, even if other people think you are strange, brings joy and pleasure. It also builds up your self-esteem because it grounds you solidly in your own personal values. This, in turn, makes you much more attractive to others. Not only that, it improves your relationships immeasurably, because you are living authentically and not betraying yourself by trying to prove your worth to others by being something you are not.

Glittering Venus, the brightest planet in the heavens, was named after the goddess of love, war and victory. Earlier names for her were Aphrodite, Innana and Ishtar. She was beautiful, self-willed and self-indulgent but was also skilled in all the arts of civilisation.

Your Venus sign shows what you desire and would like to possess, not only in relationships but also in all aspects of your taste, from clothes and culture to hobbies and hobby-horses. It identifies how and where you can be charming and seductive and skilful at creating your own type of beauty yourself. It also describes your style of attracting partners and the kind of people that turn you on. When your Venus is activated you feel powerful, desirable and wonderfully, wickedly indulged and indulgent. When it is not, even if someone has all the right credentials to make a good match, the relationship will always lack that certain something. If you don't take the chance to express your Venus to a good enough degree somewhere in your life, you miss out woefully on delight and happiness.

Morning Star, Evening Star

Venus appears in the sky either in the morning or in the evening. The ancients launched their attacks when Venus became a morning star, believing that she was then in her warrior-goddess role, releasing aggressive energy for victory in battle. If you're a morning-star person, you're likely to be impulsive, self-willed and idealistic, prepared to hold out until you find the partner who is just right for you.

Relationships and business dealings of morning-star Venus people are said to prosper best whenever Venus in the sky is a morning star. If you are an early bird, you can check this out. At these times Venus can be seen in the eastern sky before the Sun has risen.

The name for Venus as an evening star is Hesperus and it was then, traditionally, said to be sacred to lovers. Evening-star people tend to be easy-going and are open to negotiation, conciliation and making peace. If you are an evening-star Venus person, your best times in relationship and business affairs are said to be when Venus can be seen, jewel-like, in the western sky after the Sun has set.

Because the orbit of Venus is so close to the Sun, your Venus can only be in one of five signs. You have a morning-star Venus if your Venus is in one of the two signs that come before your Sun sign in the zodiac. You have an evening-star Venus if your Venus is in either of the two signs that follow your Sun sign. If you have Venus in the same sign as your Sun, you could be either, depending on whether your Venus is ahead of or behind your Sun. (You can find out which at the author's website www.janeridderpatrick.com.)

If you don't yet know your Venus sign, you might like to read through all of the following descriptions and see if you can guess what it is. You can find out for sure on pp. 116–18

At the beginning of each section are the names of some well-known Pisceans with that particular Venus sign. You can find out more about them in Chapter Ten, Famous Pisces Birthdays.

Sun in Pisces with Venus in Aries

Robert Baden-Powell	Jilly Cooper	Edward Kennedy
Nick Leeson	Elizabeth Taylor	Valentina Tereshkova

Adventure, daring and danger are just the things to lift your spirits and you can find yourself drawn like a magnet to wherever there is conflict, risk or even violence, in real life or in fiction. It's essential that you find some kind of more suitable outlet for your restless and dynamic energies than Nick Leeson, who lost $1.3 billion of his employer's money in risky investments that could have netted him $27 billion – but didn't. Robert Baden-Powell, who founded the Boy Scouts to give boys a taste of adventure and independence, might be a better role model. Challenging projects you can pour your heart into, then leave behind once you've cracked them, are ideal for you.

Volatile and impulsive, you can fall head over heels in love and then out of it again with remarkable speed. An incurable romantic, no matter how often love has let you down, the hope that this time you have found the Real Thing will never desert you. With little patience or subtlety, you could plunge straight into a relationship, and sometimes even marriage, giving very little thought to the long-term implications or practicalities of the situation. It pays to wait until the flames of passion die down before making a commitment. Especially tempting as partners are people who are suffering. You can then see yourself as the hero or heroine who has to rush to the rescue. You tend to be attracted to strong, feisty, independent types who bring colour, and sometimes trouble, into your life. You've a tendency to try to dominate but are never quite able to, and that's the way you like it. Any partner who would submit to your control would never earn or keep your respect.

Sun in Pisces with Venus in Taurus

Juliette Binoche	Luther Burbank	Prince Edward
James Taylor	Nigel Lawson	Harold Wilson

Being security-conscious, you feel happiest in stable and familiar surroundings and with a well-lined bank account. Looking after resources, either financial or natural, can give you great pleasure. Some with this combination are drawn to economics, like prime minister Harold Wilson, who was a financial expert, and former Chancellor of the Exchequer, Nigel Lawson. You may prefer, like Luther Burbank, to align yourself with the slow rhythms of nature. He worked for 50 years, on four small acres, improving the quality of plants, and introducing over 800 new varieties, with the altruistic aim of increasing the world's food supply. In California, his birthday is celebrated as Arbor Day, and trees are planted in his memory.

As you've a heightened sense of beauty and music, art and all of the finer things in life can give you joy, as do the sensual pleasures of the body. Juliette Binoche's character in *Chocolat* celebrated the link between compassion and sweetness that you know so well. Once you commit to a relationship, unless things go badly wrong, you do so for eternity, as stability and permanence are of the utmost importance. A life without quality sex could be difficult for you. Being old-fashioned at heart, you love to spoil your loved ones with tangible demonstrations of affection – gifts, flowers and chocolates, as well as back rubs and bear hugs. A reliable and trustworthy partner suits you best, one who you know will always be there for you. Take care, though, not to try to control, or even domineer, those you love and, at all costs, avoid treating them as your possessions. Your need for familiarity can mean you stay in a relationship out of habit when love has long vanished, but even that can give you quiet satisfaction.

Sun in Pisces with Venus in Capricorn

Prince Andrew	Cindy Crawford	Sandie Shaw
Steve Jobs	Anton Mosimann	Jeanne Louise Calment

Your self-esteem is tied up with feeling accepted and approved of by people you respect and look up to, whether they are parents, bosses or those at the top of whatever ladder you'd like to ascend. You love people, objects and customs that evoke a sense of history. Carrying on the traditions of your community can give you great satisfaction. This could be something as simple as wearing a family heirloom at your wedding, or as elevated as being an official dignitary of your company or country. Contentment comes from doing your duty responsibly and you love passing on your experience to those who come after you. As your work is so tied up with your pleasure, there's often no clear boundary between the one and the other, so be careful not to become a workaholic and miss out on fun.

Having long-term goals that you work towards steadily can be one of life's great pleasures. You've a shrewd business instinct, as had Jeanne Louise Calment, who died in 1997 aged 122. The lawyer who bought her flat, promising to pay her $500 a month until she died, ended up paying three times the market value for the property. 'Sometimes in life one makes bad deals,' she commented, but that would rarely apply to her – or you. You'll tend to go into contracts with your eyes wide open and some Pisceans with this placement are tempted to marry for money, position and personal gain. Marriages may be made in heaven, but you know that it takes effort on earth to keep them going. Relationships often bring with them heavy responsibilities, or restrictions, which could help ground and mature you. Partners who are sensible, socially acceptable, hard-working and ambitious are best for you.

Sun in Pisces with Venus in Aquarius

James Goldsmith	Ann Lee	Michel de Montaigne
Ronald Searle	Sharon Stone	Ivana Trump

Being a nonconformist, you may get a kick out of being contrary, just for the hell of it. Sharon Stone feels it's important to be willing to say yes, no matter who says no, and to say no, regardless of who says yes. Financier James Goldsmith openly ran a wife and a mistress at the same time, flaunting convention and appearing not to give a toss what anyone thought or said. Warm, friendly companionship is often more to your liking than hot, steamy passion and you can seem quite detached. Powerful emotions, especially of the dark and dangerous kind, and too much intimacy, can make you run for cover. Being part of an experimental or humanitarian group can bring you great pleasure. Ann Lee, who founded the Shakers in 1774, preached celibacy and equality between men and women.

Friends mean a great deal to you, and if they are ever in trouble you are a friend indeed. The French essayist

Montaigne wrote: 'I am better at friendship than anything else.' For a long-lasting commitment, a like-minded partner who shares your ideas and ideals – and gives you space – is a must. Your pleasures and tastes can be out of the ordinary and your dress sense quite outrageous. The notion of restraint in personal adornment never seems to have occurred to Ivana Trump. Like cartoonist Ronald Searle, you may indulge a quirky sense of humour and revel in life's absurdities. You are likely to be skilled at networking and even if you never see people you care for from one end of a decade to another, or they live at the opposite side of the world, you will still feel connected. It is the meeting of minds that matters, not their close physical presence.

Sun in Pisces with Venus in Pisces

| Jack Kerouac | Edgar Cayce | George Harrison |
| Elizabeth Barrett Browning | Vera Lynn | Anaïs Nin |

You can be drawn to people who need rescuing or fixing, who then become dependent or irresponsible – and not as attentive to your needs as you'd like. You may prefer to stay ostrich-like about the hard realities of relating and keep on searching for the prince, or princess, who will make your fantasies come true and magic away all of your suffering. It may even happen. Elizabeth Barrett was whisked away from her domineering father, and the reclusive life of an invalid, by fellow poet Robert Browning. You can take bittersweet pleasure in the exquisite agonies of unrequited love, or in falling for people who are unavailable. The medium Edgar Cayce had a deep soul connection with his secretary, but the relationship was never consummated.

Once the magic and allure of a new partner has worn off, you can be left faintly disappointed and yearning for . . . well, you're not quite sure what. You are, however, capable of devoted, sometimes self-sacrificial and deeply spiritual love. You may also have difficulty in saying 'no' to other people's emotional demands, or to romantic temptations – and be led astray by hard-luck stories or a good seductive line. It's easy to confuse sympathy with love and hard not to use your talent for helping and healing to attract others, rather than looking honestly at your own emotional needs and ensuring you get those satisfied. Beauty, art, music and devotional meditation can uplift and soothe you, for the true source of your happiness lies in being transported out of yourself and just blissfully drifting as if in the womb, with no responsibility or conflict. You'd rather spend your last few pence on hyacinths for the soul than a new pair of shoes (unless, of course, they were from Manolo Blahnik).

TEN

Famous Pisces Birthdays

FIND OUT WHO SHARES YOUR MOON, MERCURY AND VENUS SIGNS, and any challenging Sun aspects, and see what they have done with the material they were born with. Notice how often it is not just the personalities of the people themselves but the roles of actors, characters of authors and works of artists that reflect their astrological make-up. In reading standard biographies, I've been constantly astounded – and, of course, delighted – at how often phrases used to describe individuals could have been lifted straight from their astrological profiles. Check it out yourself!

A few people below have been given a choice of two Moons. This is because the Moon changed sign on the day that they were born and no birth time was available. You may be able to guess which one is correct if you read the descriptions of the Moon signs in Chapter Seven.

19 February
1473 Nicolaus Copernicus, astronomer who proposed that the Sun was the centre of the universe
Sun aspects: Saturn, Pluto
Moon: Sagittarius   Mercury: Pisces   Venus: Aries

20 February
1927 Sidney Poitier, first black superstar, *Guess Who's Coming to Dinner*
Sun aspects: Saturn, Neptune
Moon: Libra   Mercury: Pisces   Venus: Pisces

21 February
1937 Jilly Cooper, wickedly witty popular novelist, *Polo*, *Riders*
Sun aspects: none
Moon: Cancer   Mercury: Aquarius   Venus: Aries

22 February
1732 George Washington, first US president
Sun aspects: Uranus
Moon: Capricorn   Mercury: Aquarius   Venus: Pisces

23 February
1685 George Friedrich Handel, composer, best-known for his *Messiah*
Sun aspects: Saturn
Moon: Pisces   Mercury: Aquarius   Venus: Aquarius

24 February
1786 Wilhelm Grimm, compiler of fairy tales, *Hansel and Gretel*, *Snow White*
Sun aspects: none
Moon: Capricorn   Mercury: Aquarius   Venus: Aquarius

25 February
1861 Rudolph Steiner, mystic, philosopher and founder of Steiner schools
Sun aspects: Saturn, Uranus
Moon: Virgo   Mercury: Pisces   Venus: Aquarius

26 February
1802 Victor Hugo, author, *Les Misérables*
Sun aspects: Saturn, Pluto
Moon: Sagittarius   Mercury: Pisces   Venus: Pisces

27 February
1932 Elizabeth Taylor, much-married actress, *Who's Afraid of Virginia Woolf?*
Sun aspects: Neptune
Moon: Scorpio   Mercury: Pisces   Venus: Aries

28 February
1901 Linus Pauling, Nobel Prize-winning physicist and promoter of vitamin C
Sun aspects: Uranus, Pluto
Moon: Cancer   Mercury: Pisces   Venus: Aquarius

29 February
1916 Dinah Shore, first woman star to have her own prime-time TV variety show
Sun aspects: none
Moon: Capricorn   Mercury: Aquarius   Venus: Aries

1 March
1810 Frédéric Chopin, romantic Polish composer
Sun aspects: Saturn, Neptune, Pluto
Moon: Capricorn   Mercury: Aquarius   Venus: Pisces

2 March
1931 Mikhail Gorbachev, Soviet leader who brought about peace with the West
Sun aspects: Neptune
Moon: Leo   Mercury: Aquarius   Venus: Capricorn

3 March
1847 Alexander Graham Bell, inventor of the telephone
Sun aspects: Saturn
Moon: Virgo   Mercury: Pisces   Venus: Aries

4 March
1678 Antonio Vivaldi, composer, *The Four Seasons*
Sun aspects: none
Moon: Leo   Mercury: Aquarius   Venus: Aries

5 March
1908 Rex Harrison, actor, *My Fair Lady*
Sun aspects: Pluto
Moon: Aries   Mercury: Pisces   Venus: Aries

6 March
1475 Michelangelo, sculptor and painter of the ceiling of the Sistine Chapel
Sun aspects: Pluto
Moon: Pisces   Mercury: Aquarius   Venus: Aries

7 March
1875 Maurice Ravel, composer, *Bolero*
Sun aspects: none
Moon: Pisces   Mercury: Pisces   Venus: Aquarius

8 March
1859 Kenneth Grahame, children's author, *The Wind in the Willows*
Sun aspects: Neptune
Moon: Aries/Taurus   Mercury: Pisces   Venus: Aquarius

9 March
1934 Yuri Gagarin, first person to travel in space
Sun aspects: Neptune
Moon: Sagittarius   Mercury: Pisces   Venus: Aquarius

10 March
1964 Prince Edward, third son of Queen Elizabeth II
Sun aspects: Pluto
Moon: Aquarius   Mercury: Pisces   Venus: Taurus

11 March
1952 Douglas Adams, author, *The Hitchhiker's Guide to the Galaxy*
Sun aspects: none
Moon: Virgo   Mercury: Aries   Venus: Aquarius

12 March
1946 Liza Minnelli, singer and actress, *Cabaret*
Sun aspects: Uranus
Moon: Cancer   Mercury: Aries   Venus: Aries

13 March
1911 L. Ron Hubbard, science fiction writer and founder of Scientology
Sun aspects: Pluto
Moon: Virgo   Mercury: Pisces   Venus: Aries

14 March
1879 Albert Einstein, physicist who proposed the theories of relativity and the formula $E=mc^2$
Sun aspects: none
Moon: Sagittarius   Mercury: Aries   Venus: Aries

15 March
1779 Lord Melbourne, former prime minister and adviser to Queen Victoria
Sun aspects: Uranus, Neptune
Moon: Aquarius   Mercury: Pisces   Venus: Aquarius

16 March
1926 Jerry Lewis, actor and comedian, *The Nutty Professor*
Sun aspects: Uranus
Moon: Taurus   Mercury: Aries   Venus: Aquarius

17 March
1919 Nat 'King' Cole, romantic singer, 'Ramblin' Rose', 'Too Young'
Sun aspects: Pluto
Moon: Libra   Mercury: Aries   Venus: Aries

18 March
1869 Neville Chamberlain, former British prime minister who tried to appease Hitler
Sun aspects: none
Moon: Taurus   Mercury: Aquarius   Venus: Pisces

19 March
1813 David Livingstone, medical missionary and explorer
Sun aspects: Pluto
Moon: Scorpio   Mercury: Aries   Venus: Pisces

20 March
1917 Vera Lynn, singer known as the 'Forces' sweetheart' during the Second World War
Sun aspects: Pluto
Moon: Aquarius   Mercury: Pisces   Venus: Pisces

Other Piscean people mentioned in this book
Ansel Adams, black-and-white photographer of Yosemite National Park ☆ Prince Andrew, second son of Queen Elizabeth II ☆ W.H. Auden, poet, *Another Time* ☆ Pam Ayers, poet, *My Husband* ☆ Robert Baden-Powell, founder of the Boy Scout movement ☆ Douglas Bader, Second World War heroic fighter pilot ☆ Elizabeth Barrett Browning, poet, *The Cry of the Children* ☆ Drew Barrymore, actress, *Charlie's Angels* ☆ Cyrano de Bergerac, French writer, *Voyages to the Sun and Moon* ☆ Juliette Binoche, actress, *The English Patient* ☆ Gordon Brown, Labour Chancellor of the Exchequer ☆ Luther Burbank, horticulturist who developed new strains of fruits and vegetables ☆ Sir Richard Burton, explorer who translated *The Arabian Nights* ☆ Lady Isabel Burton, adventurous wife of Sir Richard Burton ☆ Michael Caine, actor, *The Italian Job* ☆ Jeanne Louise Calment, oldest person ever recorded ☆ Edgar Cayce, trance medium known as 'The Sleeping Prophet' ☆ Glenn Close, actress, *101 Dalmatians* ☆ Kurt Cobain, drug-fuelled guitarist of Nirvana who killed himself ☆ Robin Cook, Labour politician ☆ Emile Coué, French self-help hypnotist ☆ Cindy Crawford, entrepreneurial supermodel ☆ Adelle Davis, controversial nutritionist, *Let's Eat Right to Keep Fit* ☆ Lawrence Durrell, author, *Justine, Balthazar, Mountolive, Clea* ☆ Sir Ranulph Fiennes, explorer and expedition leader, *Living Dangerously* ☆ Galileo Galilei, astronomer persecuted by the Inquisition as a heretic ☆ James Goldsmith, charismatic financier and founder of the Referendum Party ☆ Calouste Gulbenkian, oil magnate and art collector who left $70

million for a foundation to support the arts, social welfare and education ☆ Neil Hamilton, ex-politician accused of sleaze ☆ Sheila Hancock, actress, *Buster* ☆ Jean Harlow, blonde Hollywood legend, *Bombshell* ☆ George Harrison, guitarist of The Beatles, 'My Sweet Lord' ☆ Patty Hearst, kidnapped heiress turned bank-robber ☆ Steve Jobs, founder of Apple Macintosh computers ☆ Kiri Te Kanawa, New Zealand opera singer who sang at Prince Charles' wedding ☆ Edward Kennedy, US politician whose life has been dogged by scandal and tragedy ☆ Jack Kerouac, beatnik poet and writer, *On the Road* ☆ Robin Knox-Johnston, first person to sail single-handedly round the world ☆ Nigel Lawson, Chancellor of the Exchequer under Margaret Thatcher ☆ Ann Lee, visionary founder of the Shaker sect ☆ Nick Leeson, rogue trader who caused the biggest financial collapse in banking history ☆ John Leslie, TV personality accused and cleared of rape ☆ Miriam Makeba, singer and civil-rights activist ☆ Josef Mengele, Nazi doctor who experimented cruelly on twins ☆ Michaelangelo, artist and sculptor, *David* ☆ Liza Minnelli, singer and actress, *Cabaret* ☆ Michel de Montaigne, French man of letters, *Essays* ☆ Patrick Moore, astronomer and TV presenter, *The Sky at Night* ☆ Anton Mosimann, top chef who founded cuisine naturelle ☆ Rupert Murdoch, media magnate, *The Times*, Sky TV ☆ Ralph Nader, environmental campaigner ☆ Anaïs Nin, French diarist and erotic writer ☆ Pat Nixon, wife of former US president Richard Nixon ☆ Rudolph Nureyev, Russian ballet dancer who partnered Margot Fonteyn ☆ Boris Pasternak, Russian poet and author, *Doctor Zhivago* ☆ Samuel Pepys, diarist who recorded the Great Plague and the Great Fire of London ☆ Yitzhak Rabin, assassinated Israeli prime minister ☆ James Redfield, New Age writer, *The Celestine Prophecy* ☆ Lynn Redgrave, actress, *Georgy Girl* ☆ Miranda Richardson, actress, *Damage* ☆ Willie Rodger, Scottish artist and printmaker, *Wee Kiss* ☆ Philip Roth, author,

Goodbye Columbus ☆ Baron Rothschild, German rabbi and financier ☆ Vita Sackville-West, poet, novelist, gardener and model for Virginia Woolf's *Orlando* ☆ Arthur Schopenhauer, philosopher, *The World as Will and Idea* ☆ Ronald Searle, cartoonist of *St Trinian's* schoolgirls ☆ Ariel Sharon, Israeli prime minister ☆ Sandie Shaw, singer, 'Puppet on a String' ☆ Karen Silkwood, activist portrayed by Meryl Streep in *Silkwood* ☆ Nina Simone, singer, 'Young, Gifted and Black' ☆ Lord Snowdon, photographer once married to Princess Margaret ☆ John Steinbeck, author, *Of Mice and Men* ☆ Sharon Stone, actress, *Basic Instinct* ☆ Lytton Strachey, writer who transformed the art of biography ☆ Levi Strauss, creator of jeans ☆ James Taylor, singer, 'Sweet Baby James' ☆ Valentina Tereshkova, first woman in space ☆ Ellen Terry, the greatest Shakespearean actress of her day ☆ Ivana Trump, model and ex-wife of property tycoon Donald Trump ☆ Julie Walters, actress, *Billy Elliot* ☆ Kenneth Williams, actor of snooty roles in the *Carry On* films ☆ Harold Wilson, former British Labour prime minister ☆ Joanne Woodward, actress married to Paul Newman since 1958, *Three Faces of Eve*.

ELEVEN

Finding your Sun, Moon, Mercury and Venus Signs

ALL OF THE ASTROLOGICAL DATA IN THIS BOOK WAS CALCULATED by Astrolabe, who also supply a wide range of astrological software. I am most grateful for their help and generosity.

ASTROLABE, PO Box 1750, Brewster, MA 02631, USA
www.alabe.com

PLEASE NOTE THAT ALL OF THE TIMES GIVEN ARE IN GREENWICH MEAN TIME (GMT). If you were born during British Summer Time (BST) you will need to subtract one hour from your birth time to convert it to GMT. If you were born outside of the British Isles, find the time zone of your place of birth and the number of hours it is different from GMT. Add the difference in hours if you were born west of the UK, and subtract the difference if you were born east of the UK to convert your birth time to GMT.

Your Sun Sign

Check your year of birth, and if you were born between the dates and times given the Sun was in Pisces when you were born – confirming that you're a Piscean. If you were born before the time on the date that Pisces begins in your year, you are an Aquarian. If you were born after the time on the date Pisces ends in your year, you are an Arien.

Your Moon Sign

The Moon changes sign every two and a half days. To find your Moon sign, first find your year of birth. You will notice that in each year box there are three columns.

The second column shows the day of the month that the Moon changed sign, while the first column gives the abbreviation for the sign that the Moon entered on that date.

In the middle column, the month has been omitted, so that the dates run from, for example, 18 to 28 (February) and then from 1 to 21 (March).

In the third column, after the star, the time that the Moon changed sign on that day is given.

Look down the middle column of your year box to find your date of birth. If your birth date is given, look to the third column to find the time that the Moon changed sign. If you were born after that time, your Moon sign is given in the first column next to your birth date. If you were born before that time, your Moon sign is the one above the one next to your birth date.

If your birth date is not given, find the closest date before it. The sign shown next to that date is your Moon sign.

If you were born on a day that the Moon changed signs and you do not know your time of birth, try out both of that day's Moon signs and feel which one fits you best.

The abbreviations for the signs are as follows:

Aries – Ari   Taurus – Tau   Gemini – Gem   Cancer – Can
Leo – Leo   Virgo – Vir   Libra – Lib   Scorpio – Sco
Sagittarius – Sag Capricorn – Cap   Aquarius – Aqu   Pisces – Pis

Your Mercury Sign

Find your year of birth and then the column in which your birthday falls. Look up to the top of the column to find your Mercury sign. You will see that some dates appear twice. This is because Mercury changed sign that day. If your birthday falls on one of these dates, try out both Mercury signs and see which one fits you best. If you know your birth time, you can find out for sure which Mercury sign is yours on my website – www.janeridderpatrick.com.

Your Venus Sign

Find your year of birth and then the column in which your birthday falls. Look up to the top of the column to find your Venus sign. Some dates have two possible signs. That's because Venus changed signs that day. Try them both out and see which fits you best. If the year you are interested in doesn't appear in the tables, or you have Venus in the same sign as your Sun and want to know whether you have a morning or evening star Venus, you can find the information on my website – www.janeridderpatrick.com.

♓ Pisces Sun Tables ☉

YEAR	PISCES BEGINS	PISCES ENDS
1930	19 Feb 08.50	21 Mar 08.29
1931	19 Feb 14.40	21 Mar 14.06
1932	19 Feb 20.28	20 Mar 19.53
1933	19 Feb 20.28	20 Mar 19.53
1934	19 Feb 08.01	21 Mar 07.28
1935	19 Feb 13.52	21 Mar 13.17
1936	19 Feb 19.33	20 Mar 18.57
1937	19 Feb 01.20	21 Mar 00.45
1938	19 Feb 07.19	21 Mar 06.43
1939	19 Feb 13.09	21 Mar 12.28
1940	19 Feb 19.03	20 Mar 18.23
1941	19 Feb 00.56	21 Mar 00.20
1942	19 Feb 06.46	21 Mar 06.10
1943	19 Feb 12.40	21 Mar 12.02
1944	19 Feb 18.27	20 Mar 17.48
1945	19 Feb 00.14	20 Mar 23.37
1946	19 Feb 06.08	21 Mar 05.32
1947	19 Feb 11.51	21 Mar 11.12
1948	19 Feb 17.36	20 Mar 16.56
1949	18 Feb 23.27	20 Mar 22.48
1950	19 Feb 05.17	21 Mar 04.35
1951	19 Feb 11.09	21 Mar 10.25
1952	19 Feb 16.56	20 Mar 16.13
1953	18 Feb 22.41	20 Mar 22.00
1954	19 Feb 04.32	21 Mar 03.53
1955	19 Feb 10.18	21 Mar 09.35
1956	19 Feb 16.04	20 Mar 15.20
1957	18 Feb 21.58	20 Mar 21.16
1958	19 Feb 03.48	21 Mar 03.05
1959	19 Feb 09.37	21 Mar 08.54
1960	19 Feb 15.26	20 Mar 14.42
1961	18 Feb 21.16	20 Mar 20.32
1962	19 Feb 03.14	21 Mar 02.29
1963	19 Feb 09.08	21 Mar 08.19

YEAR	PISCES BEGINS	PISCES ENDS
1964	19 Feb 14.57	20 Mar 14.09
1965	18 Feb 20.47	20 Mar 20.04
1966	19 Feb 02.37	21 Mar 01.53
1967	19 Feb 08.23	21 Mar 07.36
1968	19 Feb 14.09	20 Mar 13.22
1969	18 Feb 19.54	20 Mar 19.08
1970	19 Feb 01.41	21 Mar 00.56
1971	19 Feb 07.27	21 Mar 06.38
1972	19 Feb 13.11	20 Mar 12.21
1973	18 Feb 19.01	20 Mar 18.12
1974	19 Feb 00.58	21 Mar 00.06
1975	19 Feb 06.49	21 Mar 05.56
1976	19 Feb 12.39	20 Mar 11.49
1977	18 Feb 18.30	20 Mar 17.42
1978	19 Feb 00.21	20 Mar 23.33
1979	19 Feb 06.13	21 Mar 05.22
1980	19 Feb 12.01	20 Mar 11.09
1981	18 Feb 17.51	20 Mar 17.02
1982	18 Feb 23.46	20 Mar 22.55
1983	19 Feb 05.30	21 Mar 04.38
1984	19 Feb 11.16	20 Mar 10.24
1985	18 Feb 17.07	20 Mar 16.13
1986	18 Feb 22.57	20 Mar 22.02
1987	19 Feb 04.50	21 Mar 03.52
1988	19 Feb 10.35	20 Mar 09.38
1989	18 Feb 16.20	20 Mar 15.28
1990	18 Feb 22.14	20 Mar 21.19
1991	19 Feb 03.58	21 Mar 03.02
1992	19 Feb 09.43	20 Mar 08.48
1993	18 Feb 15.35	20 Mar 14.40
1994	18 Feb 21.21	20 Mar 20.28
1995	19 Feb 03.10	21 Mar 08.03
1996	19 Feb 09.00	20 Mar 08.03
1997	18 Feb 14.51	20 Mar 13.54
1998	18 Feb 20.54	20 Mar 19.54
1999	19 Feb 02.46	21 Mar 01.45
2000	19 Feb 08.33	20 Mar 07.35

✶ Pisces – Finding Your Moon Sign ☽

1930		
Sag	20	*06:48
Cap	22	*18:12
Aqu	25	*06:56
Pis	27	*19:12
Ari	2	*06:08
Tau	4	*15:18
Gem	6	*22:14
Can	9	*02:33
Leo	11	*04:25
Vir	13	*04:53
Lib	15	*05:43
Sco	17	*08:47
Sag	19	*15:24

1931		
Ari	20	*06:20
Tau	22	*18:53
Gem	25	*05:12
Can	27	*11:45
Leo	1	*14:24
Vir	3	*14:20
Lib	5	*13:32
Sco	7	*14:03
Sag	9	*17:30
Cap	12	*00:39
Aqu	14	*11:03
Pis	16	*23:26
Ari	19	*12:23

1932		
Leo	19	*19:48
Vir	21	*22:24
Lib	23	*23:21
Sco	26	*00:20
Sag	28	*02:39
Cap	1	*07:06
Aqu	3	*14:00
Pis	5	*23:15
Ari	8	*10:35
Tau	10	*23:19
Gem	13	*12:02
Can	15	*22:44
Leo	18	*05:55

1933		
Cap	19	*19:22
Aqu	21	*22:29
Pis	24	*02:56
Ari	26	*09:42
Tau	28	*19:20
Gem	3	*07:17
Can	5	*19:42
Leo	8	*06:17
Vir	10	*13:40
Lib	12	*18:02
Sco	14	*20:27
Sag	16	*22:18
Cap	19	*00:47

1934		
Tau	18	*17:03
Gem	21	*02:17
Can	23	*14:22
Leo	26	*03:13
Vir	28	*14:45
Lib	3	*00:01
Sco	5	*06:58
Sag	7	*11:57
Cap	9	*15:21
Aqu	11	*17:35
Pis	13	*19:25
Ari	15	*22:00
Tau	18	*02:46

♓ Pisces – Finding Your Moon Sign ☽

1935		
Vir	18	*13:32
Lib	21	*02:02
Sco	23	*13:03
Sag	25	*21:39
Cap	28	*03:03
Aqu	2	*05:15
Pis	4	*05:13
Ari	6	*04:40
Tau	8	*05:43
Gem	10	*10:12
Can	12	*18:51
Leo	15	*06:47
Vir	17	*19:51
Lib	20	*08:07

1936		
Cap	18	*08:20
Aqu	20	*12:45
Pis	22	*13:54
Ari	24	*13:34
Tau	26	*13:51
Gem	28	*16:30
Can	1	*22:26
Leo	4	*07:20
Vir	6	*18:17
Lib	9	*06:25
Sco	11	*19:03
Sag	14	*07:05
Cap	16	*16:51
Aqu	18	*22:50

1937		
Gem	18	*05:22
Can	20	*09:04
Leo	22	*13:51
Vir	24	*20:04
Lib	27	*04:26
Sco	1	*15:23
Sag	4	*04:07
Cap	6	*16:22
Aqu	9	*01:34
Pis	11	*06:49
Ari	13	*08:59
Tau	15	*09:53
Gem	17	*11:19
Can	19	*14:25

1938		
Sco	19	*11:38
Sag	21	*22:34
Cap	24	*11:27
Aqu	26	*23:34
Pis	1	*09:12
Ari	3	*16:15
Tau	5	*21:28
Gem	8	*01:32
Can	10	*04:45
Leo	12	*07:22
Vir	14	*10:05
Lib	16	*14:08
Sco	18	*20:54

1939		
Pis	19	*08:51
Ari	21	*20:22
Tau	24	*06:18
Gem	26	*13:46
Can	28	*18:06
Leo	2	*19:29
Vir	4	*19:16
Lib	6	*19:25
Sco	8	*22:00
Sag	11	*04:23
Cap	13	*14:35
Aqu	16	*03:01
Pis	18	*15:31

♓ Pisces – Finding Your Moon Sign ☽

1940

Can	19	*01:44
Leo	21	*04:18
Vir	23	*04:11
Lib	25	*03:29
Sco	27	*04:14
Sag	29	*07:55
Cap	2	*15:03
Aqu	5	*01:07
Pis	7	*13:07
Ari	10	*02:00
Tau	12	*14:43
Gem	15	*01:51
Can	17	*09:55
Leo	19	*14:13

1941

Sag	18	*18:36
Cap	20	*22:54
Aqu	23	*05:01
Pis	25	*13:18
Ari	27	*23:54
Tau	2	*12:23
Gem	5	*01:11
Can	7	*12:02
Leo	9	*19:18
Vir	11	*22:50
Lib	13	*23:50
Sco	16	*00:03
Sag	18	*01:08

1942

Tau	20	*07:57
Gem	22	*19:47
Can	25	*08:15
Leo	27	*19:05
Vir	2	*03:05
Lib	4	*08:22
Sco	6	*11:49
Sag	8	*14:28
Cap	10	*17:08
Aqu	12	*20:30
Pis	15	*01:09
Ari	17	*07:41
Tau	19	*16:38

1943

Vir	20	*04:19
Lib	22	*14:29
Sco	24	*22:24
Sag	27	*03:58
Cap	1	*07:18
Aqu	3	*08:55
Pis	5	*09:54
Ari	7	*11:42
Tau	9	*15:53
Gem	11	*23:40
Can	14	*10:51
Leo	16	*23:40
Vir	19	*11:42

1944

Cap	19	*17:32
Aqu	21	*19:26
Pis	23	*19:08
Ari	25	*18:30
Tau	27	*19:36
Gem	1	*00:07
Can	3	*08:38
Leo	5	*20:19
Vir	8	*09:18
Lib	10	*21:54
Sco	13	*09:11
Sag	15	*18:30
Cap	18	*01:12

♓ Pisces – Finding Your Moon Sign ☽

1945		
Gem	19	*08:01
Can	21	*13:43
Leo	23	*21:58
Vir	26	*08:13
Lib	28	*19:56
Sco	3	*08:32
Sag	5	*20:44
Cap	8	*06:37
Aqu	10	*12:38
Pis	12	*14:48
Ari	14	*14:31
Tau	16	*13:54
Gem	18	*15:05
Can	20	*19:31

1946		
Lib	18	*17:36
Sco	21	*04:05
Sag	23	*16:40
Cap	26	*05:01
Aqu	28	*14:33
Pis	2	*20:24
Ari	4	*23:22
Tau	7	*01:08
Gem	9	*03:12
Can	11	*06:28
Leo	13	*11:14
Vir	15	*17:32
Lib	18	*01:40
Sco	20	*12:05

1947		
Aqu	18	*12:37
Pis	20	*22:56
Ari	23	*06:57
Tau	25	*13:07
Gem	27	*17:46
Can	1	*20:58
Leo	3	*22:59
Vir	6	*00:46
Lib	8	*03:51
Sco	10	*09:51
Sag	12	*19:34
Cap	15	*08:00
Aqu	17	*20:34
Pis	20	*06:57

1948		
Gem	18	*04:55
Can	20	*09:07
Leo	22	*10:06
Vir	24	*09:22
Lib	26	*09:05
Sco	28	*11:25
Sag	1	*17:41
Cap	4	*03:50
Aqu	6	*16:14
Pis	9	*04:52
Ari	11	*16:32
Tau	14	*02:39
Gem	16	*10:44
Can	18	*16:13
Leo	20	*18:57

1949		
Sag	19	*22:50
Cap	22	*05:50
Aqu	24	*15:26
Pis	27	*02:54
Ari	1	*15:35
Tau	4	*04:32
Gem	6	*16:04
Can	9	*00:19
Leo	11	*04:32
Vir	13	*05:23
Lib	15	*04:39
Sco	17	*04:25
Sag	19	*06:30

♓ Pisces – Finding Your Moon Sign ☽

1950		
Ari	19	*13:01
Tau	22	*01:11
Gem	24	*14:02
Can	27	*01:01
Leo	1	*08:29
Vir	3	*12:23
Lib	5	*13:59
Sco	7	*14:55
Sag	9	*16:37
Cap	11	*20:07
Aqu	14	*01:52
Pis	16	*09:59
Ari	18	*20:21

1951		
Leo	19	*08:00
Vir	21	*16:42
Lib	23	*23:00
Sco	26	*03:30
Sag	28	*06:49
Cap	2	*09:29
Aqu	4	*12:10
Pis	6	*15:45
Ari	8	*21:16
Tau	11	*05:32
Gem	13	*16:36
Can	16	*05:05
Leo	18	*16:44

1952		
Sag	18	*19:41
Cap	20	*22:48
Aqu	22	*23:47
Pis	25	*00:01
Ari	27	*01:12
Tau	29	*05:01
Gem	2	*12:37
Can	4	*23:40
Leo	7	*12:29
Vir	10	*00:50
Lib	12	*11:15
Sco	14	*19:20
Sag	17	*01:14
Cap	19	*05:19

1953		
Tau	18	*09:51
Gem	20	*14:28
Can	22	*22:48
Leo	25	*10:05
Vir	27	*22:50
Lib	2	*11:40
Sco	4	*23:30
Sag	7	*09:19
Cap	9	*16:09
Aqu	11	*19:36
Pis	13	*20:16
Ari	15	*19:38
Tau	17	*19:44
Gem	19	*22:36

1954		
Lib	20	*09:14
Sco	22	*21:43
Sag	25	*09:59
Cap	27	*19:56
Aqu	2	*02:05
Pis	4	*04:31
Ari	6	*04:39
Tau	8	*04:32
Gem	10	*06:06
Can	12	*10:38
Leo	14	*18:16
Vir	17	*04:21
Lib	19	*15:57

1955		
Aqu	20	*03:32
Pis	22	*10:08
Ari	24	*14:05
Tau	26	*16:46
Gem	28	*19:23
Can	2	*22:39
Leo	5	*02:48
Vir	7	*08:09
Lib	9	*15:20
Sco	12	*01:04
Sag	14	*13:13
Cap	17	*02:00
Aqu	19	*12:45

1956		
Gem	19	*09:49
Can	21	*12:48
Leo	23	*14:10
Vir	25	*15:05
Lib	27	*17:20
Sco	29	*22:46
Sag	3	*08:09
Cap	5	*20:32
Aqu	8	*09:18
Pis	10	*20:10
Ari	13	*04:25
Tau	15	*10:31
Gem	17	*15:11
Can	19	*18:47

1957		
Sco	19	*01:07
Sag	21	*07:23
Cap	23	*17:26
Aqu	26	*05:42
Pis	28	*18:24
Ari	3	*06:30
Tau	5	*17:20
Gem	8	*02:02
Can	10	*07:44
Leo	12	*10:10
Vir	14	*10:19
Lib	16	*09:59
Sco	18	*11:15
Sag	20	*15:54

1958		
Pis	18	*16:39
Ari	21	*05:01
Tau	23	*18:04
Gem	26	*05:52
Can	28	*14:15
Leo	2	*18:26
Vir	4	*19:14
Lib	6	*18:35
Sco	8	*18:34
Sag	10	*20:57
Cap	13	*02:37
Aqu	15	*11:28
Pis	17	*22:41

1959		
Can	18	*13:49
Leo	20	*21:36
Vir	23	*02:04
Lib	25	*04:28
Sco	27	*06:14
Sag	1	*08:33
Cap	3	*12:06
Aqu	5	*17:16
Pis	8	*00:26
Ari	10	*09:54
Tau	12	*21:36
Gem	15	*10:30
Can	17	*22:26
Leo	20	*07:21

♓ Pisces – Finding Your Moon Sign ☽

1960		
Sag	19	*23:11
Cap	22	*01:39
Aqu	24	*03:32
Pis	26	*06:03
Ari	28	*10:38
Tau	1	*18:18
Gem	4	*05:07
Can	6	*17:36
Leo	9	*05:24
Vir	11	*14:46
Lib	13	*21:18
Sco	16	*01:36
Sag	18	*04:37
Cap	20	*07:14

1961		
Tau	19	*18:21
Gem	22	*01:52
Can	24	*12:49
Leo	27	*01:34
Vir	1	*14:11
Lib	4	*01:20
Sco	6	*10:22
Sag	8	*17:03
Cap	10	*21:18
Aqu	12	*23:28
Pis	15	*00:26
Ari	17	*01:32
Tau	19	*04:25

1962		
Vir	19	*12:26
Lib	22	*01:21
Sco	24	*13:35
Sag	26	*23:45
Cap	1	*06:37
Aqu	3	*09:50
Pis	5	*10:15
Ari	7	*09:32
Tau	9	*09:40
Gem	11	*12:36
Can	13	*19:25
Leo	16	*05:55
Vir	18	*18:32

1963		
Cap	19	*08:59
Aqu	21	*15:22
Pis	23	*18:17
Ari	25	*19:04
Tau	27	*19:38
Gem	1	*21:39
Can	4	*02:08
Leo	6	*09:15
Vir	8	*18:33
Lib	11	*05:34
Sco	13	*17:51
Sag	16	*06:26
Cap	18	*17:34

1964		
Tau	18	*08:44
Gem	20	*11:47
Can	22	*14:49
Leo	24	*18:10
Vir	26	*22:30
Lib	29	*04:46
Sco	2	*13:54
Sag	5	*01:46
Cap	7	*14:34
Aqu	10	*01:34
Pis	12	*09:04
Ari	14	*13:14
Tau	16	*15:29
Gem	18	*17:25
Can	20	*20:11

♓ Pisces – Finding Your Moon Sign ☽

1965		
Lib	18	*06:45
Sco	20	*11:46
Sag	22	*20:57
Cap	25	*09:17
Aqu	27	*22:13
Pis	2	*09:37
Ari	4	*18:44
Tau	7	*01:48
Gem	9	*07:13
Can	11	*11:02
Leo	13	*13:22
Vir	15	*14:55
Lib	17	*17:04
Sco	19	*21:33

1966		
Pis	20	*08:04
Ari	22	*20:29
Tau	25	*07:52
Gem	27	*17:02
Can	1	*22:46
Leo	4	*00:55
Vir	6	*00:36
Lib	7	*23:49
Sco	10	*00:48
Sag	12	*05:18
Cap	14	*13:56
Aqu	17	*01:34
Pis	19	*14:18

1967		
Can	20	*03:46
Leo	22	*08:03
Vir	24	*09:03
Lib	26	*08:44
Sco	28	*09:10
Sag	2	*11:53
Cap	4	*17:35
Aqu	7	*02:04
Pis	9	*12:41
Ari	12	*00:53
Tau	14	*13:53
Gem	17	*02:18
Can	19	*12:08

1968		
Sco	18	*21:59
Sag	21	*00:47
Cap	23	*04:12
Aqu	25	*08:37
Pis	27	*14:42
Ari	29	*23:15
Tau	3	*10:27
Gem	5	*23:16
Can	8	*11:20
Leo	10	*20:26
Vir	13	*01:50
Lib	15	*04:22
Sco	17	*05:33
Sag	19	*06:53

1969		
Ari	18	*23:49
Tau	21	*07:01
Gem	23	*17:41
Can	26	*06:11
Leo	28	*18:11
Vir	3	*04:06
Lib	5	*11:33
Sco	7	*16:56
Sag	9	*20:47
Cap	11	*23:39
Aqu	14	*02:09
Pis	16	*05:03
Ari	18	*09:27

♓ Pisces – Finding Your Moon Sign ☽

1970		
Leo	18	*14:53
Vir	21	*03:41
Lib	23	*15:29
Sco	26	*01:22
Sag	28	*08:37
Cap	2	*12:52
Aqu	4	*14:33
Pis	6	*14:48
Ari	8	*15:16
Tau	10	*17:43
Gem	12	*23:37
Can	15	*09:19
Leo	17	*21:39
Vir	20	*10:29

1971		
Sag	18	*13:44
Cap	20	*20:35
Aqu	22	*23:41
Pis	25	*00:04
Ari	26	*23:30
Tau	28	*23:55
Gem	3	*03:02
Can	5	*09:48
Leo	7	*19:55
Vir	10	*08:10
Lib	12	*21:05
Sco	15	*09:30
Sag	17	*20:22
Cap	20	*04:36

1972		
Tau	19	*11:11
Gem	21	*13:36
Can	23	*17:52
Leo	26	*00:15
Vir	28	*08:39
Lib	1	*19:00
Sco	4	*07:00
Sag	6	*19:36
Cap	9	*06:49
Aqu	11	*14:41
Pis	13	*18:39
Ari	15	*19:36
Tau	17	*19:27
Gem	19	*20:13

1973		
Lib	19	*17:58
Sco	22	*02:35
Sag	24	*14:14
Cap	27	*03:03
Aqu	1	*14:21
Pis	3	*22:29
Ari	6	*03:36
Tau	8	*06:50
Gem	10	*09:30
Can	12	*12:29
Leo	14	*16:07
Vir	16	*20:42
Lib	19	*02:48

1974		
Aqu	19	*11:20
Pis	21	*23:14
Ari	24	*09:11
Tau	26	*17:10
Gem	28	*23:09
Can	3	*02:58
Leo	5	*04:48
Vir	7	*05:33
Lib	9	*06:51
Sco	11	*10:40
Sag	13	*18:19
Cap	16	*05:41
Aqu	18	*18:38

♓ Pisces – Finding Your Moon Sign ☽

1975		
Gem	19	*07:34
Can	21	*13:16
Leo	23	*15:12
Vir	25	*14:36
Lib	27	*13:39
Sco	1	*14:34
Sag	3	*19:05
Cap	6	*03:40
Aqu	8	*15:09
Pis	11	*03:48
Ari	13	*16:18
Tau	16	*03:51
Gem	18	*13:42
Can	20	*20:47

1976		
Sco	20	*00:14
Sag	22	*03:18
Cap	24	*08:54
Aqu	26	*16:48
Pis	29	*02:41
Ari	2	*14:22
Tau	5	*03:17
Gem	7	*15:55
Can	10	*01:57
Leo	12	*07:54
Vir	14	*09:57
Lib	16	*09:44
Sco	18	*09:18

1977		
Pis	18	*04:44
Ari	20	*12:23
Tau	22	*23:06
Gem	25	*11:49
Can	28	*00:01
Leo	2	*09:23
Vir	4	*15:17
Lib	6	*18:34
Sco	8	*20:36
Sag	10	*22:42
Cap	13	*01:40
Aqu	15	*05:59
Pis	17	*12:06
Ari	19	*20:23

1978		
Leo	20	*07:09
Vir	22	*17:39
Lib	25	*02:02
Sco	27	*08:27
Sag	1	*13:01
Cap	3	*15:57
Aqu	5	*17:50
Pis	7	*19:45
Ari	9	*23:09
Tau	12	*05:18
Gem	14	*14:48
Can	17	*02:48
Leo	19	*15:11

1979		
Sag	19	*23:49
Cap	22	*03:59
Aqu	24	*05:11
Pis	26	*04:52
Ari	28	*04:54
Tau	2	*07:09
Gem	4	*12:59
Can	6	*22:34
Leo	9	*10:47
Vir	11	*23:42
Lib	14	*11:40
Sco	16	*21:48
Sag	19	*05:37

109

✻ Pisces – Finding Your Moon Sign ☽

1980		1981		1982		1983		1984	
Ari 18	*13:42	Vir 18	*22:34	Cap 18	*15:35	Tau 18	*08:29	Lib 19	*03:39
Tau 20	*14:35	Lib 21	*08:12	Aqu 21	*03:14	Gem 20	*14:50	Sco 21	*04:44
Gem 22	*17:58	Sco 23	*19:54	Pis 23	*12:07	Can 22	*18:30	Sag 23	*09:23
Can 25	*00:35	Sag 26	*08:28	Ari 25	*18:16	Leo 24	*19:46	Cap 25	*17:49
Leo 27	*10:10	Cap 28	*19:45	Tau 27	*22:31	Vir 26	*19:49	Aqu 28	*05:02
Vir 29	*21:53	Aqu 3	*03:49	Gem 2	*01:49	Lib 28	*20:30	Pis 1	*17:29
Lib 3	*10:39	Pis 5	*08:11	Can 4	*04:48	Sco 2	*23:52	Ari 4	*06:06
Sco 5	*23:22	Ari 7	*09:47	Leo 6	*07:50	Sag 5	*07:15	Tau 6	*18:08
Sag 8	*10:37	Tau 9	*10:22	Vir 8	*11:27	Cap 7	*18:29	Gem 9	*04:29
Cap 10	*19:01	Gem 11	*11:42	Lib 10	*16:34	Aqu 10	*07:29	Can 11	*11:46
Aqu 12	*23:43	Can 13	*15:06	Sco 13	*00:17	Pis 12	*19:46	Leo 13	*15:19
Pis 15	*01:09	Leo 15	*21:03	Sag 15	*11:03	Ari 15	*06:00	Vir 15	*15:46
Ari 17	*00:40	Vir 18	*05:19	Cap 17	*23:46	Tau 17	*14:03	Lib 17	*14:51
Tau 19	*00:13	Lib 20	*15:30	Aqu 20	*11:51	Gem 19	*20:19	Sco 19	*14:49

♓ Pisces – Finding Your Moon Sign ☽

1985		
Pis	19	*16:38
Ari	22	*03:42
Tau	24	*16:27
Gem	27	*05:10
Can	1	*15:22
Leo	3	*21:26
Vir	5	*23:41
Lib	7	*23:47
Sco	9	*23:47
Sag	12	*01:29
Cap	14	*05:54
Aqu	16	*13:11
Pis	18	*22:50

1986		
Leo	21	*22:23
Vir	24	*04:57
Lib	26	*09:06
Sco	28	*12:05
Sag	2	*14:51
Cap	4	*17:55
Aqu	6	*21:42
Pis	9	*02:48
Ari	11	*10:04
Tau	13	*20:04
Gem	16	*08:22
Can	18	*21:03
Leo	21	*07:37

1987		
Sco	19	*00:03
Sag	21	*05:08
Cap	23	*07:56
Aqu	25	*09:08
Pis	27	*10:07
Ari	1	*12:37
Tau	3	*18:11
Gem	6	*03:26
Can	8	*15:24
Leo	11	*03:54
Vir	13	*14:54
Lib	15	*23:33
Sco	18	*05:56

1988		
Ari	19	*18:35
Tau	21	*20:51
Gem	24	*02:43
Can	26	*12:12
Leo	29	*00:12
Vir	2	*13:06
Lib	5	*01:31
Sco	7	*12:26
Sag	9	*20:57
Cap	12	*02:30
Aqu	14	*05:07
Pis	16	*05:41
Ari	18	*05:45
Tau	20	*07:05

1989		
Leo	18	*00:33
Vir	20	*11:34
Lib	23	*00:04
Sco	25	*12:56
Sag	28	*00:28
Cap	2	*08:56
Aqu	4	*13:35
Pis	6	*14:58
Ari	8	*14:36
Tau	10	*14:25
Gem	12	*16:16
Can	14	*21:28
Leo	17	*06:12
Vir	19	*17:39

♓ Pisces – Finding Your Moon Sign ☽

1990		
Cap	20	*08:29
Aqu	22	*16:51
Pis	24	*21:48
Ari	27	*00:15
Tau	1	*01:42
Gem	3	*03:37
Can	5	*07:02
Leo	7	*12:25
Vir	9	*19:47
Lib	12	*05:08
Sco	14	*16:25
Sag	17	*04:56
Cap	19	*17:01

1991		
Tau	19	*14:23
Gem	21	*18:10
Can	23	*20:56
Leo	25	*23:12
Vir	28	*01:50
Lib	1	*06:03
Sco	4	*13:09
Sag	6	*23:35
Cap	9	*12:13
Aqu	12	*00:29
Pis	14	*10:09
Ari	16	*16:37
Tau	18	*20:40
Gem	20	*23:36

1992		
Vir	18	*09:46
Lib	20	*10:05
Sco	22	*13:12
Sag	24	*20:26
Cap	27	*07:33
Aqu	29	*20:33
Pis	3	*09:10
Ari	5	*20:06
Tau	8	*05:04
Gem	10	*12:02
Can	12	*16:49
Leo	14	*19:20
Vir	16	*20:13
Lib	18	*20:55
Sco	20	*23:21

1993		
Aqu	18	*19:05
Pis	21	*07:11
Ari	23	*19:50
Tau	26	*08:11
Gem	28	*18:51
Can	3	*02:14
Leo	5	*05:40
Vir	7	*05:52
Lib	9	*04:46
Sco	11	*04:40
Sag	13	*07:34
Cap	15	*14:28
Aqu	18	*00:52
Pis	20	*13:10

1994		
Gem	18	*18:05
Can	21	*04:26
Leo	23	*10:46
Vir	25	*13:26
Lib	27	*14:05
Sco	1	*14:43
Sag	3	*16:53
Cap	5	*21:24
Aqu	8	*04:15
Pis	10	*13:09
Ari	12	*23:59
Tau	15	*12:27
Gem	18	*01:28
Can	20	*12:52

♓ Pisces – Finding Your Moon Sign ☽

1995		
Sco	20	*03:54
Sag	22	*07:12
Cap	24	*10:10
Aqu	26	*13:14
Pis	28	*17:15
Ari	2	*23:30
Tau	5	*08:50
Gem	7	*20:55
Can	10	*09:39
Leo	12	*20:27
Vir	15	*03:53
Lib	17	*08:17
Sco	19	*10:51

1996		
Pis	19	*00:09
Ari	21	*01:59
Tau	23	*07:08
Gem	25	*16:14
Can	28	*04:10
Leo	1	*16:46
Vir	4	*04:12
Lib	6	*13:39
Sco	8	*21:04
Sag	11	*02:31
Cap	13	*06:07
Aqu	15	*08:14
Pis	17	*09:50
Ari	19	*12:16

1997		
Leo	19	*13:52
Vir	22	*02:38
Lib	24	*15:22
Sco	27	*02:56
Sag	1	*11:59
Cap	3	*17:38
Aqu	5	*19:53
Pis	7	*19:56
Ari	9	*19:32
Tau	11	*20:38
Gem	14	*00:49
Can	16	*08:51
Leo	18	*20:08

1998		
Sag	19	*13:55
Cap	21	*22:28
Aqu	24	*03:09
Pis	26	*04:41
Ari	28	*04:41
Tau	2	*05:00
Gem	4	*07:15
Can	6	*12:27
Leo	8	*20:46
Vir	11	*07:35
Lib	13	*19:57
Sco	16	*08:50
Sag	18	*20:55

1999		
Ari	18	*15:05
Tau	20	*17:28
Gem	22	*19:53
Can	24	*23:09
Leo	27	*03:44
Vir	1	*10:05
Lib	3	*18:34
Sco	6	*05:22
Sag	8	*17:45
Cap	11	*05:53
Aqu	13	*15:31
Pis	15	*21:29
Ari	18	*00:11
Tau	20	*01:08

2000		
Vir	19	*15:53
Lib	21	*19:21
Sco	24	*01:58
Sag	26	*12:10
Cap	29	*00:45
Aqu	2	*13:13
Pis	4	*23:28
Ari	7	*06:53
Tau	9	*12:00
Gem	11	*15:45
Can	13	*18:51
Leo	15	*21:43
Vir	18	*00:48
Lib	20	*04:57

♓ Pisces Mercury Signs ☿

YEAR	AQUARIUS	PISCES	ARIES
1930	18 Feb–9 Mar	9 Mar–21 Mar	
1931	18 Feb–2 Mar	2 Mar–18 Mar	18 Mar–21 Mar
1932	18 Feb–23 Feb	23 Feb–9 Mar	9 Mar–21 Mar
1933		18 Feb–3 Mar	3 Mar–21 Mar
1934		18 Feb–21 Mar	
1935	18 Feb–18 Mar	18 Mar–21 Mar	
1936	18 Feb–13 Mar	13 Mar–21 Mar	
1937	18 Feb–6 Mar	6 Mar–21 Mar	
1938	18 Feb–27 Feb	27 Feb–15 Mar	15 Mar–21 Mar
1939		18 Feb–7 Mar	7 Mar–21 Mar
1940		18 Feb–4 Mar	4 Mar–21 Mar
1941	7 Mar–16 Mar	18 Feb–7 Mar	
		16 Mar–21 Mar	
1942	18 Feb–17 Mar	17 Mar–21 Mar	
1943	18 Feb–11 Mar	11 Mar–21 Mar	
1944	18 Feb–3 Mar	3 Mar–19 Mar	19 Mar–21 Mar
1945	18 Feb–23 Feb	23 Feb–11 Mar	11 Mar–21 Mar
1946		18 Feb–4 Mar	4 Mar–21 Mar
1947		18 Feb–21 Mar	
1948	20 Feb–18 Mar	19 Feb–20 Feb	
		18 Mar–20 Mar	
1949	18 Feb–14 Mar	14 Mar–21 Mar	
1950	18 Feb–7 Mar	7 Mar–21 Mar	
1951	18 Feb–28 Feb	28 Feb–16 Mar	16 Mar–21 Mar
1952	19 Feb–20 Feb	20 Feb–7 Mar	7 Mar–21 Mar
1953		18 Feb–2 Mar	·2 Mar–15 Mar
		15 Mar–21 Mar	
1954		18 Feb–21 Mar	
1955	18 Feb–17 Mar	17 Mar–21 Mar	
1956	18 Feb–11 Mar	11 Mar–21 Mar	
1957	18 Feb–4 Mar	4 Mar–20 Mar	20 Mar
1958	18 Feb–24 Feb	24 Feb–12 Mar	12 Mar–21 Mar
1959		18 Feb–5 Mar	5 Mar–21 Mar
1960		18 Feb–21 Mar	
1961	24 Feb–18 Mar	18 Feb–24 Feb	
		18 Mar–21 Mar	
1962	18 Feb–15 Mar	15 Mar–21 Mar	
1963	18 Feb–9 Mar	9 Mar–21 Mar	
1964	18 Feb–29 Feb	29 Feb–16 Mar	16 Mar–21 Mar
1965	18 Feb–21 Feb	21 Feb–9 Mar	9 Mar–21 Mar

YEAR	AQUARIUS	PISCES	ARIES
1966		18 Feb–3 Mar	3 Mar–21 Mar
1967		18 Feb–21 Mar	
1968	18 Feb–17 Mar	17 Mar–21 Mar	
1969	18 Feb–12 Mar	12 Mar–21 Mar	
1970	18 Feb–5 Mar	5 Mar–21 Mar	
1971	18 Feb–26 Feb	26 Feb–14 Mar	14 Mar–21 Mar
1972		18 Feb–5 Mar	5 Mar–21 Mar
1973		18 Feb–21 Mar	
1974	2 Mar–17 Mar	18 Feb–2 Mar	
		17 Mar–21 Mar	
1975	18 Feb–16 Mar	16 Mar–21 Mar	
1976	18 Feb–9 Mar	9 Mar–21 Mar	
1977	18 Feb–2 Mar	2 Mar–18 Mar	18 Mar–21 Mar
1978	18 Feb–22 Feb	22 Feb–10 Mar	10 Mar–21 Mar
1979		18 Feb–3 Mar	3 Mar–21 Mar
1980		18 Feb–21 Mar	
1981	18 Feb–18 Mar	18 Mar–21 Mar	
1982	18 Feb–13 Mar	13 Mar–21 Mar	
1983	18 Feb–7 Mar	7 Mar–21 Mar	
1984	18 Feb–27 Feb	27 Feb–14 Mar	14 Mar–21 Mar
1985		18 Feb–7 Mar	7 Mar–21 Mar
1986		18 Feb–3 Mar	3 Mar–11 Mar
		11 Mar–21 Mar	
1987	12 Mar–13 Mar	18 Feb–12 Mar	
		13 Mar–21 Mar	
1988	18 Feb–16 Mar	16 Mar–21 Mar	
1989	18 Feb–10 Mar	10 Mar–21 Mar	
1990	18 Feb–3 Mar	3 Mar–21 Mar	21 Mar
1991	18 Feb–24 Feb	24 Feb–11 Mar	11 Mar–21 Mar
1992		18 Feb–3 Mar	3 Mar–21 Mar
1993		18 Feb–21 Mar	
1994	21 Feb–18 Mar	18 Feb–21 Feb	
		18 Mar–21 Mar	
1995	18 Feb–14 Mar	14 Mar–21 Mar	
1996	18 Feb–7 Mar	7 Mar–21 Mar	
1997	18 Feb–28 Feb	28 Feb–16 Mar	16 Mar–21 Mar
1998	18 Feb–20 Feb	20 Feb–8 Mar	8 Mar–21 Mar
1999		18 Feb–2 Mar	2 Mar–18 Mar
		18 Mar–21 Mar	
2000		18 Feb–21 Mar	

♓ Pisces Venus Signs ♀

YEAR	CAPRICORN	AQUARIUS	PISCES	ARIES	TAURUS
1930			18 Feb–12 Mar	12 Mar–21 Mar	
1931	18 Feb–5 Mar'	5 Mar–21 Mar			
1932				18 Feb–9 Mar	9 Mar–21 Mar
1933		18 Feb–3 Mar	3 Mar–21 Mar		
1934		18 Feb–21 Mar			
1935			18 Feb–26 Feb	26 Feb–21 Mar	
1936	18 Feb–22 Feb	22 Feb–17 Mar	17 Mar–21 Mar		
1937				18 Feb–9 Mar	9 Mar–21 Mar
1938			18 Feb–12 Mar	12 Mar–21 Mar	
1939	18 Feb–8 Mar	8 Mar–21 Mar			
1940				18 Feb–8 Mar	8 Mar–21 Mar
1941		18 Feb–2 Mar	2 Mar–21 Mar		
1942		18 Feb–21 Mar			
1943			18 Feb–25 Feb	25 Feb–21 Mar	
1944	18 Feb–21 Feb	21 Feb–17 Mar	17 Mar–21 Mar		
1945				18 Feb–11 Mar	11 Mar–21 Mar
1946			18 Feb–11 Mar	11 Mar–21 Mar	
1947	18 Feb–5 Mar	5 Mar–21 Mar			
1948				18 Feb–8 Mar	8 Mar–21 Mar
1949		18 Feb–2 Mar	2 Mar–21 Mar		
1950		18 Feb–21 Mar			
1951			18 Feb–24 Feb	24 Feb–21 Mar	

YEAR	CAPRICORN	AQUARIUS	PISCES	ARIES	TAURUS
1952	18 Feb–21 Feb	21 Feb–16 Mar	16 Mar–21 Mar	18 Feb–14 Mar	14 Mar–21 Mar
1953			18 Feb–11 Mar	11 Mar–21 Mar	
1954					
1955	18 Feb–4 Mar	4 Mar–21 Mar		18 Feb–7 Mar	7 Mar–21 Mar
1956			1 Mar–21 Mar		
1957		18 Feb–1 Mar			
1958		18 Feb–21 Mar			
1959	19 Feb–20 Feb	20 Feb–16 Mar	18 Feb–24 Feb	24 Feb–21 Mar	21 Mar
1960			16 Mar–20 Mar		
1961				18 Feb–21 Mar	
1962			18 Feb–10 Mar	10 Mar–21 Mar	
1963	18 Feb–4 Mar	4 Mar–21 Mar		18 Feb–7 Mar	7 Mar–21 Mar
1964			1 Mar–21 Mar		
1965					
1966	18 Feb–25 Feb	18 Feb–1 Mar	18 Feb–23 Feb		
1967		25 Feb–21 Mar	15 Mar–21 Mar	23 Feb–21 Mar	21 Mar
1968	19 Feb	20 Feb–15 Mar		18 Feb–21 Mar	
1969			18 Feb–10 Mar	10 Mar–21 Mar	
1970					
1971	18 Feb–4 Mar	4 Mar–21 Mar		18 Feb–7 Mar	7 Mar–21 Mar
1972			28 Feb–21 Mar		
1973		18 Feb–28 Feb			
1974	18 Feb–28 Feb	28 Feb–21 Mar			
1975			18 Feb–23 Feb	23 Feb–19 Mar	
1976		18 Feb–15 Mar	15 Mar–21 Mar		19 Mar–21 Mar

YEAR	CAPRICORN	AQUARIUS	PISCES	ARIES	TAURUS
1977				18 Feb–21 Mar	
1978				9 Mar–21 Mar	
1979	18 Feb–3 Mar	3 Mar–21 Mar	18 Feb–9 Mar	18 Feb–6 Mar	6 Mar–21 Mar
1980					
1981	18 Feb–2 Mar	18 Feb–28 Feb	28 Feb–21 Mar		
1982		2 Mar–21 Mar			
1983			18 Feb–22 Feb	22 Feb–19 Mar	19 Mar–21 Mar
1984		18 Feb–14 Mar	14 Mar–21 Mar		
1985				18 Feb–21 Mar	
1986				9 Mar–21 Mar	
1987	18 Feb–3 Mar	3 Mar–21 Mar	18 Feb–9 Mar	18 Feb–6 Mar	6 Mar–21 Mar
1988					
1989	18 Feb–3 Mar	18 Feb–27 Feb	27 Feb–21 Mar		
1990		3 Mar–21 Mar			
1991			18 Feb–22 Feb	22 Feb–18 Mar	18 Mar–21 Mar
1992		18 Feb–13 Mar	13 Mar–21 Mar		
1993				18 Feb–21 Mar	
1994			18 Feb–8 Mar	8 Mar–21 Mar	
1995	19 Feb–2 Mar	2 Mar–21 Mar			
1996					
1997		18 Feb–27 Feb	27 Feb–21 Mar	18 Feb–6 Mar	6 Mar–21 Mar
1998	18 Feb–4 Mar	4 Mar–21 Mar			
1999			18 Feb–21 Feb	21 Feb–18 Mar	18 Mar–21 Mar
2000		18 Feb–13 Mar	13 Mar–21 Mar		

The Pisces Workbook

There are no right or wrong answers in this chapter. Its aim is to help you assess how you are doing with your life – in YOUR estimation – and to make the material of this book more personal and, I hope, more helpful for you.

1. The Pisces in You
Which of the following Pisces characteristics do you recognise in yourself?

healing	rescuing	glamorous
spiritual	compassionate	empathetic
intuitive	understanding	idealistic
romantic	artistic	going with the flow

2. In which situations do you find yourself acting like this?

_____

_____

3. When you are feeling vulnerable you may show some of the less constructive Pisces traits. Do you recognise yourself in any of the following?

helpless	evasive	martyred
reclusive	deceptive	masochistic
dependent	hypersensitive	emotionally fragile

What kind of situations trigger off this behaviour and what do you think might help you, in these situations, to respond more positively?

_____

_____

4. You and Your Roles
a) Where, if anywhere, in your life do you play the role of Dreamer?

_____

_____

b) Whom, or what, do you dream of?

_____

_____

5. Do you play any of the following roles – in the literal or broad sense – in any part of your life? If not, would you like to? What might be your first step towards doing so?

Rescuer   Artist   Poet
Mystic   Redeemer   Healer

_____

_____

6. Sun Aspects
If any of the following planets aspects your Sun, add each of the keywords for that planet to complete the following sentences. Which phrases ring true for you?

I am _____

My father is_____

My job requires that I am_____

Saturn Words (Use only if your Sun is aspected by Saturn)

ambitious	controlling	judgmental	mature
serious	strict	traditional	bureaucratic
cautious	committed	hard-working	disciplined
depressive	responsible	status-seeking	limiting

Uranus Words (Use only if your Sun is aspected by Uranus)

freedom-loving	progressive	rebellious	shocking
scientific	cutting-edge	detached	contrary
friendly	disruptive	eccentric	humanitarian
innovative	nonconformist	unconventional	exciting

Neptune Words (Use only if your Sun is aspected by Neptune)

sensitive	idealistic	artistic	impressionable
disappointing	impractical	escapist	self-sacrificing
spiritual	unrealistic	dreamy	glamorous
dependent	deceptive	rescuing	blissful

Pluto Words (Use only if your Sun is aspected by Pluto)

powerful	single-minded	intense	extreme
secretive	rotten	passionate	mysterious
investigative	uncompromising	ruthless	wealthy
abusive	regenerative	associated with sex, birth or death	

a) If one or more negative words describe you or your job, how might you turn that quality into something more positive or satisfying?

_____

_____

7. The Moon and You

Below are brief lists of what the Moon needs, in the various elements, to feel secure and satisfied. First find your Moon element, then estimate how much of each of the following you are expressing and receiving in your life, especially at home and in your relationships, on a scale of 0 to 5 where 0 = none and 5 = plenty.

FIRE MOONS — Aries, Leo, Sagittarius

attention	action	drama
recognition	self-expression	spontaneity
enthusiasm	adventure	leadership

EARTH MOONS — Taurus, Virgo, Capricorn

stability	orderly routine	sensual pleasures
material security	a sense of rootedness	control over your home life
regular body care	practical achievements	pleasurable practical tasks

AIR MOONS — Gemini, Libra, Aquarius

mental rapport	stimulating ideas	emotional space
friendship	social justice	interesting conversations
fairness	socialising	freedom to circulate

WATER MOONS — Cancer, Scorpio, Pisces

intimacy	a sense of belonging	emotional rapport
emotional safety	respect for your feelings	time and space to retreat
acceptance	cherishing and being cherished	warmth and comfort

a) Do you feel your Moon is being 'fed' enough?

yes _____ no _____

b) How might you satisfy your Moon needs even better?

_____

_____

8. You and Your Mercury

As a Pisces, your Mercury can only be in Aquarius, Pisces or Aries. Below are some of the ways and situations in which Mercury in each of the elements might learn and communicate effectively. First find your Mercury sign, then circle the words you think apply to you.

Mercury in Fire (Aries)

| action | imagination | identifying with the subject matter |
| excitement | drama | playing with possibilities |

Mercury in Earth (As a Pisces, you can never have Mercury in an earth sign; the words are included here for completeness)

| time-tested methods | useful facts | well-structured information |
| 'how to' instructions | demonstrations | hands-on experience |

Mercury in Air (Aquarius)

| facts arranged in categories | logic | demonstrable connections |
| rational arguments | theories | debate and sharing of ideas |

Mercury in Water (Pisces)

| pictures and images | charged atmospheres | feeling-linked information |
| intuitive understanding | emotional rapport | being shown personally |

a) This game with Mercury can be done with a friend or on your own. Skim through a magazine until you find a picture that interests you. Then describe the picture – to your friend, or in writing or on tape. Notice what you emphasise and the kind of words you use. Now try to describe it using the language and emphasis of each of the other Mercury modes. How easy did you find that? Identifying the preferred Mercury style of others and using that style yourself can lead to improved communication all round.

9. Your Venus Values

Below are lists of qualities and situations that your Venus sign might enjoy. Assess on a scale of 0 to 5 how much your Venus desires and pleasures are met and expressed in your life. 0 = not at all, 5 = fully.

Venus in Aries

You will activate your Venus by taking part in anything that makes you feel potent, for example:

taking the initiative	competition	risk-taking
action dramas	taking the lead	tough challenges

Venus in Taurus

You will activate your Venus through whatever pleases the senses and enhances your sense of stability, for example:

financial security	beauty	gardening and nature
sensual pleasures	good food	body pampering

Venus in Capricorn

You will activate your Venus through anything that makes you feel a respected member of the community, for example:

doing your duty	upholding tradition	working towards goals
achieving ambitions	heading a dynasty	acquiring social status

Venus in Aquarius

You will activate your Venus through freedom from the restraints of convention, for example:

sharing progressive ideas	unusual relationships	being nonconformist
humanitarian projects	teamwork	eccentric fashions

Venus in Pisces

You will activate your Venus through anything that allows you to experience fusion with something greater than yourself, for example:

relieving suffering	daydreaming	creating a glamorous image
spiritual devotion	voluntary service	losing yourself in art, music or love

a) How, and where, might you have more fun and pleasure by bringing more of what your Venus sign loves into your life?

_____

_____

b) Make a note here of the kind of gifts your Venus sign would love to receive. Then go on and spoil yourself . . .

_____

_____

Resources

Finding an Astrologer

I'm often asked what is the best way to find a reputable astrologer. Personal recommendation by someone whose judgement you trust is by far the best way. Ideally, the astrologer should also be endorsed by a reputable organisation whose members adhere to a strict code of ethics, which guarantees confidentiality and professional conduct.

Contact Addresses

Association of Professional Astrologers
www.professionalastrologers.org

APA members adhere to a strict code of professional ethics.

Astrological Association of Great Britain
www.astrologicalassociation.co.uk

The main body for astrology in the UK that also has information on astrological events and organisations throughout the world.

Faculty of Astrological Studies
www.astrology.org.uk

The teaching body internationally recognised for excellence in astrological education at all levels.

Your Pisces Friends

You can keep a record of Pisces you know here, with the page numbers of where to find their descriptions handy for future reference.

Name _____ Date of Birth _____

Aspects★	None	Saturn	Uranus	Neptune	Pluto
Moon Sign _____				p _____	
Mercury Sign _____				p _____	
Venus Sign _____				p _____	

Name _____ Date of Birth _____

Aspects★	None	Saturn	Uranus	Neptune	Pluto
Moon Sign _____				p _____	
Mercury Sign _____				p _____	
Venus Sign _____				p _____	

Name _____ Date of Birth _____

Aspects★	None	Saturn	Uranus	Neptune	Pluto
Moon Sign _____				p _____	
Mercury Sign _____				p _____	
Venus Sign _____				p _____	

Name _____ Date of Birth _____

Aspects★	None	Saturn	Uranus	Neptune	Pluto
Moon Sign _____				p _____	
Mercury Sign _____				p _____	
Venus Sign _____				p _____	

★ Circle where applicable

Sign Summaries

SIGN	GLYPH	APPROX DATES	SYMBOL	ROLE	ELEMENT	QUALITY	PLANET	GLYPH	KEYWORD
1. Aries	♈	21/3 – 19/4	Ram	Hero	Fire	Cardinal	Mars	♂	Assertiveness
2. Taurus	♉	20/4 – 20/5	Bull	Steward	Earth	Fixed	Venus	♀	Stability
3. Gemini	♊	21/5 – 21/6	Twins	Go-Between	Air	Mutable	Mercury	☿	Communication
4. Cancer	♋	22/6 – 22/7	Crab	Caretaker	Water	Cardinal	Moon	☽	Nurture
5. Leo	♌	23/7 – 22/8	Lion	Performer	Fire	Fixed	Sun	☉	Glory
6. Virgo	♍	23/8 – 22/9	Maiden	Craftworker	Earth	Mutable	Mercury	☿	Skill
7. Libra	♎	23/9 – 22/10	Scales	Architect	Air	Cardinal	Venus	♀	Balance
8. Scorpio	♏	23/10 – 23/11	Scorpion	Survivor	Water	Fixed	Pluto	♇	Transformation
9. Sagittarius	♐	22/11 – 21/12	Archer	Adventurer	Fire	Mutable	Jupiter	♃	Wisdom
10. Capricorn	♑	22/12 – 19/1	Goat	Manager	Earth	Cardinal	Saturn	♄	Responsibility
11. Aquarius	♒	20/1 – 19/2	Waterbearer	Scientist	Air	Fixed	Uranus	♅	Progress
12. Pisces	♓	20/2 – 20/3	Fishes	Dreamer	Water	Mutable	Neptune	♆	Universality